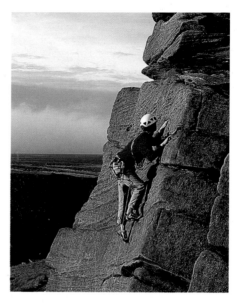

Rock climbing
moving up the grades

Rock climbing
moving up the grades

Expert techniques to take your skills to new levels

Malcolm Creasey

with
Nigel Shepherd
Nick Banks
Neil Gresham
and Ray Wood

southwater

This edition is published by Southwater

Southwater is an imprint of
Anness Publishing Limited
Hermes House
88–89 Blackfriars Road
London SE1 8HA
tel. 020 7401 2077
fax 020 7633 9499

Distributed in the UK by
The Manning Partnership
251–253 London Road East
Batheaston
Bath BA1 7RL
tel. 01225 852 727
fax 01225 852 852

Distributed in the USA by
Anness Publishing Inc.
27 West 20th Street
Suite 504
New York, NY 10011
tel. 212 807 6739
fax 212 807 6813

Distributed in Australia by
Sandstone Publishing
Unit 1, 360 Norton Street
Leichhardt
New South Wales 2040
tel. 02 9560 7888
fax 02 9560 7488

1 3 5 7 9 10 8 6 4 2

Publisher: JOANNA LORENZ
Senior Editorial Manager: JUDITH SIMONS
Consultant Editor: NEIL CHAMPION
Project Editor: MARIANO KÄLFORS
US Consultant: BOB DURAND
Designer: LISA TAI
Location Photographer: RAY WOOD
Studio Photographer: MARK DUNCALF
Illustrator: GEORGE MANLEY
Production Controller: YOLANDE DENNY
Editorial Reader: JONATHAN MARSHALLL

Previously published as part of a larger compendium,
The Complete Rock Climber

The authors and publisher wish to stress that they strongly advise the use of a helmet in all climbing situations. However,
some of the photographs in this book show people climbing without one. Similarly, some photographs show instances of
people a long way above the ground without a rope and harness. There are no laws or regulations governing the sport
(except at indoor walls and on instructional courses); climbing and mountaineering are all about self-reliance and taking
responsibility for your own decisions and actions.

Front cover image supplied by David Simmonite. Unknown climber on Goo-Goo Mak at Fraguel, Majorca.

CONTENTS

INTRODUCTION

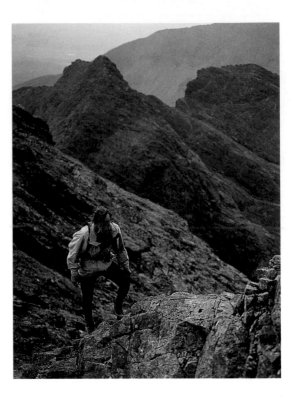

Rock climbing has been one of the fastest growing global pursuits for many years now. One need only look at the popularity of the modern phenomenon of the indoor climbing wall, as well as the growing number of climbing clubs in most towns and cities, which allows members the otherwise rare opportunity of tasting real rock.

Since it first grew out of the greater game of mountaineering, rock climbing has developed into a vast game in its own right, with many facets, its own vocabulary and unwritten rules on ethics and codes of conduct. To some extent the sport has even undergone such a degree of specialization that the term "rock climber" has become a term of generalization in danger of being rendered obsolete. Under this umbrella many different people participating in different pursuits – whether bouldering, sport-climbing, free-climbing, aid climbing or other – can group themselves. But while the sport has undergone massive changes since its humble beginnings, the spirit of fun and fair play generated by its early pioneers is still alive and very much with us to date.

Rock climbing has always been a sport with few rules, and this remains the case today. It has also carried with it from its early days the element of risk. Personal safety at an indoor climbing wall is one thing, but out on the crags, in the mountains or further afield in remote areas, it is a different matter. Personal judgement when weighing up the degree of risk involved in doing a particular climb is still an important aspect of being a competent rock climber. To some degree, these things set climbing apart from most other sports, which have set rules, generally carry far less objective risk, and do not exact such a high payment for poor judgement and decision-making.

There are many skills to be learned before anyone can claim to be a confident and competent all-round rock climber. These encompass the physical, technical and mental strengths that the sport draws on. The process of gaining new skills in each of these areas never stops. That is one of the great things about the climbing game. Even a highly experienced professional mountain guide cannot claim to know it all. But above all the sport should bring enjoyment and fulfilment to those who practise it. Each day on the rock should bring a little more fun, an opportunity to learn new skills, and a chance to explore unknown territory, either close at hand or far away. The challenges that you may choose to accept are always personal ones – they relate to your physical ability and to your own level of risk acceptance. As the level you choose to climb at progresses steadily, this book will provide you with the essential knowledge to apply safe practice and to gain more experience in this multi-faceted sport.

Above and opposite: To many rock climbers this is the ultimate challenge, where high alpine terrain after a lengthy approach has to be climbed quickly before bad weather turns it into a fight for survival.

1

ADVANCED ROCK CLIMBING

So you've left the safety of the indoor wall behind you. Most likely, your climbing has progressed to the stage where the thought of hurling yourself from bolt to bolt is only feasible these days for training purposes: getting in shape for real rock. You're completely hooked on the sport and the time has come to learn a little more about what it requires to adventure farther afield – and still be safe. You've realized that days out on the crags are not always sunny and warm affairs and, particularly in the mountains, how important it is to think and plan carefully about your equipment and preparation in terms of staying warm and dry. The advice and skills in this section will help you to cope with whatever nature and the circumstances throw at you.

Opposite: *High on a mountain crag, where problems can quickly accumulate and become serious. Do you know how to deal with them when they occur?*

Equipment for the hills

▽ There are a number of waterproof and breathable fabrics available. All do their job efficiently.

If you plan to venture farther than your local climbing wall or roadside crag, then careful consideration must be given to your clothing. Even in summer, wind and wet can create life-threatening conditions, if you are not equipped to meet them. The contents of your rucksack will make all the difference.

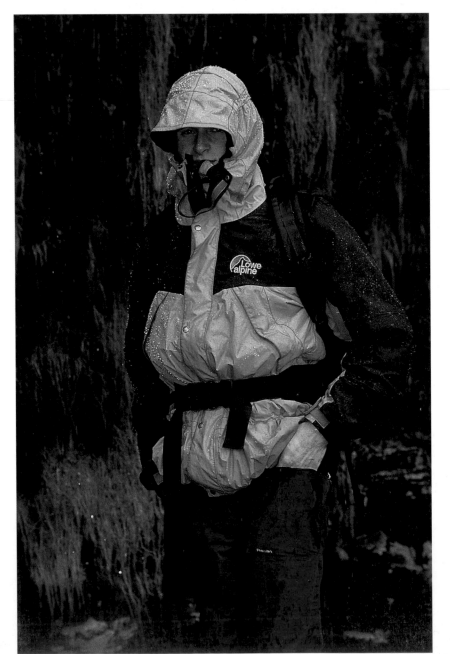

SHELL CLOTHING

The most important addition to the wardrobe is a waterproof suit of some kind. For the mountains we need something a good deal more serious. This outer layer is more often referred to as shell clothing (not to be confused with shell-suits). Fabrics and styles are varied and most climbers will opt for a waterproof and breathable fabric. The most famous of these is probably Gore-Tex™ but there are others of a similar ilk that will perform in exactly the same way. The most significant advantage this type of fabric has to offer is its ability to prevent moisture penetration from the outside but to allow moisture out from the inside, leaving the wearer warm and dry.

DESIGN FEATURES

When choosing a jacket try as many different styles on as you can. The two important aspects to consider are the overall fit and the hood. Fit is tested easily by doing up the front opening of the garment and lifting your hands above your head and stretching them out in front of you. A well-fitting jacket should not ride up over the hips nor should it stretch tightly across the back. The hood must be spacious, easy to close and, most important, should turn with the head from side to side so that your vision is not restricted.

Pockets on a jacket are a personal preference. If you need a jacket when you are climbing it is pointless having pockets at waist level or below because they will interfere with the harness. Chest pockets on a diagonal slash are probably the best. Some people like an integral map pocket inside the jacket at chest level, but unless the pockets are big enough to accommodate a map they are useless.

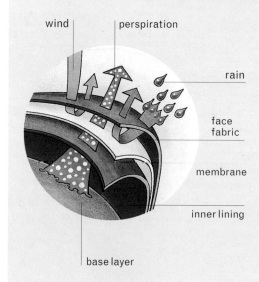

◁ *Make sure the hood of your chosen jacket will fit over the top of a helmet.*

TROUSERS

Shell pants are a must for wilder climates. Considerable heat is lost through the thigh muscles, so they should be protected. Here again, fit is very important. The most obvious aspect is that you should be able to sit in a squatting position without the pants becoming too tight and restrictive. Some people prefer a bib-and-brace type pant, while others opt for a more traditional trouser style. The bib or high-waist pant does help to keep the midriff warm, particularly in windy, snowy conditions.

▷ *All closures, particularly cuffs, should be effective and easy to use.*

◁ *Waterproof legwear is as important as a jacket, though many climbers overlook this fact.*

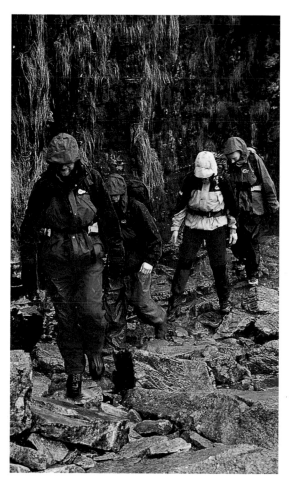

● HOW BREATHABLE FABRICS FUNCTION

wind

perspiration

rain

face fabric

membrane

inner lining

base layer

◁ *Waterproof and breathable fabrics are expensive but perform well in wet, windy weather. The special membrane contains millions of micro-pores that allow sweat to pass through, but prevent larger raindrops from entering.*

The layer system

The shell clothing that you choose forms the outer part of the layering system. This begins with a warm comfortable layer next to the skin followed by other thicker and warmer layers on top. The number of layers is entirely dependent on the outside temperature. Regardless of the number of layers you wear, try to ensure that you do not parcel yourself up too tightly for this will only limit the range of movement that you are capable of. Fortunately, modern fabrics perform extremely well and even seemingly thin layers offer effective insulation.

WINDPROOF CLOTHING

Light showerproof and windproof clothing is also worth considering. The advantages with this type of fabric are that it is inexpensive to buy and very light to carry. Garments are available that will fold up into a very small package that can be clipped on to the harness or stuffed down the front of a jumper. Unfortunately such fabrics are not terribly hardwearing and will damage easily against rough rock or sharp edges.

GLOVES AND HATS

Gloves and hat are important additions to the safety gear you'll need to carry in the mountains. Here again, weight and a combination of functionality and good design is important. You may need to wear a hat with a helmet on top. Clearly, Granny's home-knitted hat is unsuitable for this purpose. Some manufacturers offer hats that are

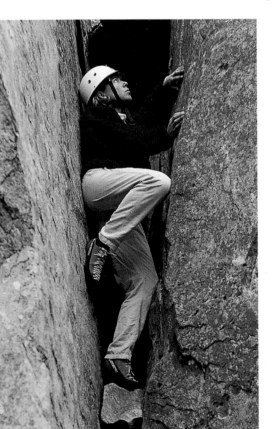

◁ Make sure that the layers of clothing you choose do not restrict movement, and that by adding subsequent outer layers you combine insulation with wind and water repellency.

▷ A basic layering system might begin with thermals and then light fleece or hardwearing fabric on top. A lightweight shell top and leggings would complete the outfit.

△ The collar of this jacket features a neck warmer that can be adjusted to a snug fit, thus retaining valuable body heat.

▷ These jackets are reversible. On one side they have a windproof material, and on the other a warm fleece layer.

close fitting and specifically designed to fit under a helmet while there are many others that will suffice. Style, colour and fashion are all influences over the choice of hat for personal use, though fleece is possibly the most practical fabric.

Gloves merit closer scrutiny. Light fleece gloves made from a fabric such as Wind-bloc™ or Windstopper™ are worth consideration. Unfortunately fleece is not terribly hardwearing, and for the occasions where you might actually want to climb with gloved hands you'll be better off having gloves with leather fingers. Though such products will be more expensive, the fact that they will last longer is a strong enough reason to sway your choice in that direction. For climbing you'll benefit from finger gloves rather than mittens. Handling gear with mittens is awkward, to say the least.

◁ A light and effective pair of gloves made with leather palms for better grip and windproof and warm fleece.

● FIRST-AID KIT

Finally, and of considerable importance, is a first-aid kit. Wherever you venture, be it 500 m (¼ mile) from the road or 50 km (30 miles) into the mountains, a first-aid kit is essential. Having cobbled one together, it is the sort of thing that can remain in the bottom of your pack until it is required. A suitable pack need not be heavy or widely comprehensive – a few plasters, wound dressings and a triangular bandage are all that's needed. Make sure that the pack is kept tightly sealed in a waterproof bag so that nothing is likely to become soaked and ruined, and periodically check the condition of the packages. It is also worth putting in a lightweight foil survival blanket and a whistle for dire emergencies.

Footwear

It is important to consider what you want your mountain footwear for – approaching a climb, where it will be taken off and exchanged for rock shoes, or wearing on an easy long route or scramble?

THE APPROACH SHOE

A simple approach walk to the crag might be undertaken in a pair of ordinary training shoes. In fact climbers have adopted this type of footwear for many years, and in response to this fact manufacturers now produce a range of footwear categorized as "approach shoes" or cross-functional footwear. There are considerable advantages in travelling to the crag in lightweight footwear, not simply because it is more comfortable. Many climbs finish high on a mountainside from which the descent might be a either a moderate walk or a difficult scramble. Clearly, rock shoes are impractical, uncomfortable and potentially lethal on such descents. A lightweight pair of shoes can be clipped on to the back of the harness where they will be barely noticed during the climb but greatly appreciated for the descent.

THE MOUNTAIN BOOT

There was a time, and not so long ago, that fully stiffened rock-climbing boots were used quite widely. While the demand for this type of boot has waned considerably, there are occasions where the benefits of a stiffer-soled boot might be advantageous. Examples of such situations include long technically easy climbs or mountaineering routes that might include the occasional

△ *Approach walks to the crags might be hot and sweaty affairs or you may feel the need to be warmer.*

◁ *Approach shoes.*

patch of snow or ice to cross. Despite the demise of the fully rigid rock-climbing boot, there is still a wide range of boots available that will fulfil these requirements and in recent years one or two manufacturers have re-introduced the specialist stiffened rock boot.

IMPORTANT CRITERIA

The important criteria to consider after comfort are the rigidity and type of sole unit. Boots that are totally rigid are uncomfortable to walk in but excellent for climbing. On the other hand a boot with considerable flex will be comfy to walk in but horrendous for rock climbing. The compromise is one that you can stand on the very tiptoe of but that still offers some support to the foot. When trying a boot on in the shop, stand on the toe on a small edge for a couple of minutes without moving. If the boot is sufficiently rigid, your foot will not tire or cramp up during this test. Boots in this category do not include plastic boots or any boot of double construction. They are usually full leather or soft Nubuck.

△ *Full-blown mountain wear for those days when you encounter a bit of everything.*

Rucksacks

A simple rucksack of rudimentary design is more than adequate for carrying gear for a short distance to the foot of a climb and back home again. However, if you intend to go farther afield, and particularly if you think you might need to carry a pack on your back while climbing, you are certain to need something much more sophisticated.

THE CLIMBING PACK

A pack that will be comfortable for climbing should conform to one or two basic design principles. Firstly, it shouldn't be too large for your needs. Avoid the temptation to go for a larger pack in the belief that it will squash down to a smaller size if it isn't full. A pack with a capacity of around 30–40 litres (7–9 gallons) should be large enough for most needs on a daily basis – after all, you only need to carry a little food and water, a light shell and maybe a spare fleece.

The pack should have no internal frame other than a padded back. It should be quite narrow so as not to restrict movement of the arms from side to side and it should be fairly short so that head movement remains unrestricted, particularly when tilting the head backwards. A teardrop-shaped pack with zip closure at the top seems to be the preferred style of day pack for rock climbing. It is also useful to have a large, strong loop at the top of the pack, which is used both as a handle and to clip the pack to the belay when it is not being carried.

▷ *A frameless rucksack of between 30–40 litres (7–9 gallons) and a rope bag. In addition to rope, the rope bag can be used to carry any extra bits of gear, as necessary.*

△ *A good pack will barely be noticed on the back. Make sure that you are not over-burdened.*

Climbing among mountains

△ *Beinn Shuas in the Scottish Highlands, a long walk in, isolation and big rewards.*

◁ *A true mountain setting. Self-reliance and all your mountaineering skills will be needed here.*

Rock climbing among the mountains is the main reason for climbing for many people. Here, it is not necessarily the technical difficulty of the climb that is important (though many mountain routes are as extreme as they come) but the special atmosphere, the solitude, the self-reliance and the companionship of a few other souls.

ADVENTURE IN THE HILLS

A sweeping sun-touched arete, crisp mountain air, snow-clad hills all around, early morning and already five pitches up. Cragging in a mountain setting is hard to beat. Rock climbing grew out of the alpinism of the Victorian era and soon developed into an entity in its own right. Until the 1960s most climbers felt that rock climbing anywhere but in a mountain setting was a cop-out or a compromise to be made if the weather was bad or you could not get to the mountains because of work or some other diversion. Roadside crags, sun-drenched sea cliffs and quarries were ok, but it

▷ *The bolt – providing sanitized and safe climbing?*

was the real thing they hankered after. The thought of hurling yourself from bolt to bolt or up and down a bit of artificial rock in a dust-filled shed was definitely beyond the comprehension of the hardy mountaineering types. The arrival of the "rock jock" was still some way off. The idea that rock climbing should be safe, warm and comfortable was beyond the grasp of climbers who had been through one, and in some cases two, world wars. Climbing was dominated by tough characters who enjoyed pitting their mental and physical wits against the mist-shrouded crags. Rain, snow, wind, falling rocks and darkness were all seen as challenges that added to the heroics and the mystique of this eccentric pastime.

SANITIZED CLIMBING?

At some stage climbers realized that it was possible to climb on solid rock using pre-placed equipment that was guaranteed to keep you safe, but most were too embarrassed to let on. It was not until sometime in the early 1980s that some of the old die-hards faltered under the influence of the "new wave" and admitted that climbing didn't have to be cold, wet, miserable and dangerous. It all made so much sense, but climbing had changed forever. It had been sanitized and made to fit in with the changing ideas of the latter part of the twentieth century.

ADVENTURE CLIMBING

What some of today's climbers now want is adrenalin rushes without the risk. Sadly, throughout the mountains of the world, climbers are bringing the mountains down to them rather than rising up to meet them. Happily though, adventure climbing still exists and its advocates guard it jealously. The challenge of adventure climbing on big mountain crags or committing sea cliffs utilizes every physical and psychological skill a climber can cobble together, and as a result provides a level of retrospective satisfaction that can make your toes wriggle with joy for months afterwards. The technical skill may be less (though not always) but the overall experience far greater than that found on a sport climb.

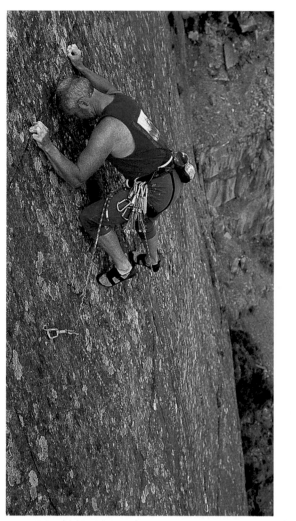

◁ A bolted sport climb will often be desperately hard but relatively safe due to the nature of the protection used.

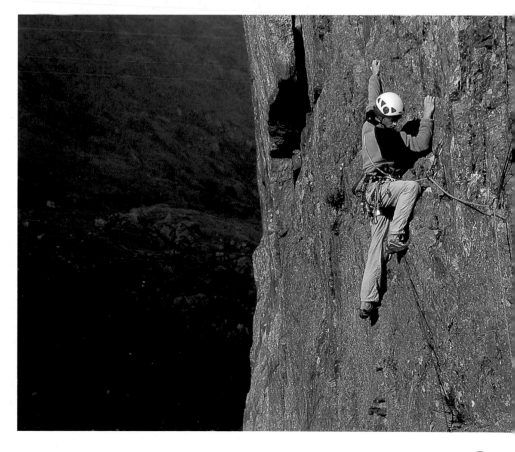

▽ The climbing may be easier, but the agenda is bigger. Placing your own protection requires planning, strength and mental coolness.

Finding your crag

Big, serious crags do not give of their pleasures easily and can give you a humbling cuff behind the ear with the greatest of ease. To sample the pleasures and to avoid the chastisement requires plenty of research, foresight and a combination of boldness and commitment that must be learnt but cannot really be taught.

MAPS AND GUIDEBOOKS

Much of the fun associated with adventure climbing lies in the anticipation and dreaming, which is bolstered by endless reading of guidebooks and climbing literature prior to setting off for the crag. Most writers hype up the accounts of climbs, so your job is to filter out the important information from the

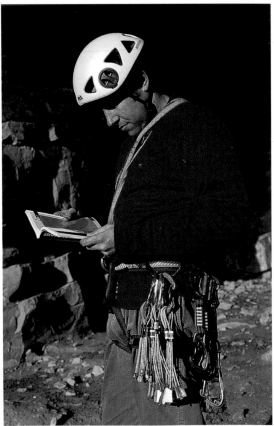

△ *Time spent ensuring that you are on the right route and your starting point is correct is time well spent. Study the guidebook well.*

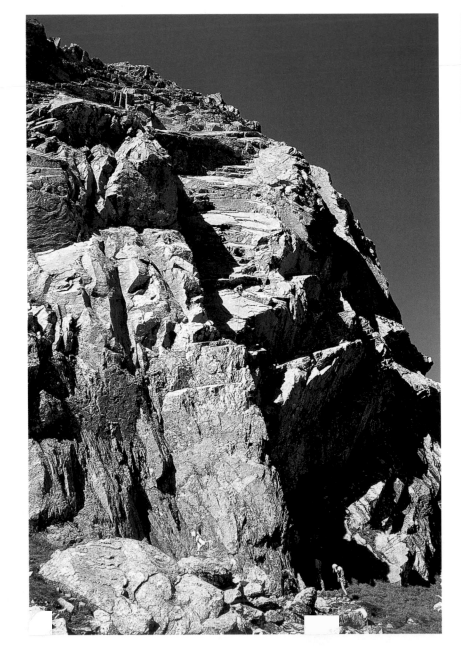

◁ *Finding your crag and finding the start of your route are often the biggest challenges in the mountains.*

▷ *Navigating accurately to your chosen mountain crag can be complex and confusing even with good weather and visibility.*

embellishment. Having settled on your crag and route, the next thing to wrestle with are the mysteries of the map. This will ensure you have a good picture of how best to get to and from the crag and what type of terrain you can expect to encounter. Interpreting maps and spotting the problems before you lurch off is an important skill. Climbers are notorious for being poor navigators but it doesn't have to be like this.

WEATHER – FRIEND AND FOE OF THE CLIMBER

On a committing crag you should always be armed with as much knowledge and information as possible, the more up-to-date the better. Rain can turn the delightful finishing groove into an unclimbable grade III rapid, an electrical storm can fry you on the spot, and nil visibility can turn the gentle descent from the crag into an epic return to the wrong valley or a night out clad only in your rock shoes and T-shirt. Conversely, you can easily spoil a perfect day by running off with your tail between your legs in the early morning cloud and drizzle, only to discover it is an inversion which burns off with the arrival of the sun to give a perfect anti-cyclonic day.

ESCAPING

If you are about to buy a one-way ticket to hell, it is best if you know this and are prepared for the consequences. Having a workable escape plan tucked up your sleeve to deal with exhaustion, changing terrain, time and weather is essential on a big crag. As you become more experienced, this can almost become subconscious; but in your early sorties it needs to be a reasonably formal exercise. Be aware that on many big routes you cannot abseil (rappel) off and your escape plan can only be to keep climbing to the top of the route.

▷ *Success is at hand, but what about getting back to the safety of the ground and rucksack?*

Adventure climbing

△ *Loose rock, poor gear and no climbing down – total commitment!*

▷ *Can you get a hand off to get the gear in? The jugs usually appear when the protection is clipped.*

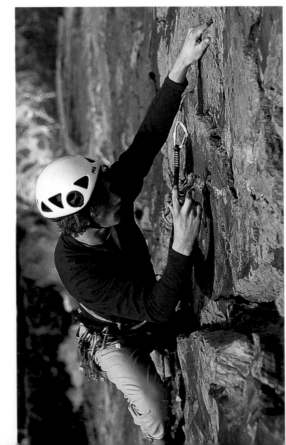

I t is the potential danger of adventure climbing and the total commitment it requires that attracts some and drives others away. If you have read this far, most likely you fall into the first camp and thrive on risk-taking and its retrospective enjoyment.

RISK ASSESSMENT

There is a big difference between making a bold dash for the glinting bolt and guaranteed safety, with the potential of retreat, and setting off up the rock ahead not knowing if any protection exists, or if it does, whether any of your diminishing rack will fit. The prospect of the perfect crack viewed from below turning out to be blind and flared, and the jug reducing to a sloper, awaits the adventure climber. Staying under control both physically and mentally in this setting is the key to successful ascents. Physical strength is obviously a great

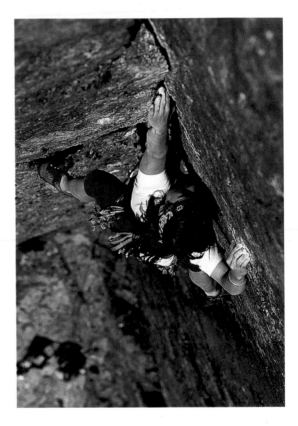

△ *Under control, with time to think and to get the protection right.*

attribute in a situation like this, but counts for little if it is not bolstered by clear foresight and a cool mind. You will notice that the placement of a good runner suddenly makes the footholds bigger and allows you to find the obvious jug around the corner — the whole thing suddenly becomes two grades easier. The trick is to create the same effect next time when the runner isn't there!

MOTIVATION

In climbing we often hear about people being "naturals". This is a nice idea, but most successful climbers emerge as a result of experience punctuated by failure, fright and constant learning. Anyone can develop the skills if they are determined enough. If there is no motivation, however, forget it. To succeed as a climber on committing crags you need to be a strange combination: selfish on one hand and a team worker on the other. The skill is to disguise the selfishness enough to avoid alienating your partner – not an easy task. It is hard to define the complex feelings that may course through your mind and body as you wind up to take on a big route. The most interesting feeling is the overpowering sense of inevitability: this climb is definitely going to happen. This should be countered by a healthy dollop of nervousness and a touch of self-doubt to balance the whole affair. Once you have set off up the rock, a sense of determination must take over. At this point the strangest things start to happen, depending on the day. They could range from one extreme to another – feeling as though you have never climbed before through to feeling as though you are on the easiest climb of your life.

SUCCESS AND RETREAT

It is important to respond to how you feel, but on a big climb you need to be able to push through the bad patches in the hope that a good one is on the way. Sometimes this just doesn't happen, so you have to either rely on your trusty partner or pack it in and go home. Backing off is an important skill for the adventure climber to develop. In Victorian times, armed with ropes that broke and no technical gear, the advice to the leader was to never climb anything that could not be reversed. Today we are blessed with equipment that allows us to abandon this approach, but we still need to be sure that the reading of the route and our forward planning allows us to bail out if need be or face the consequences. The real skill is to develop an awareness of when you have reached the point of no return, however you decide to proceed. There is a delicate and frustrating balance between recklessly hurling yourself at a problem and boldly climbing something right on the edge of your ability. If we always got it right, however, there would no adventure in adventure climbing.

▷ *Desperate moves and sustained climbing wait for you on mountain crags as well as on sport routes and roadside crags.*

▽ *Big, bold and desperate. Isolation as well as beauty in Ireland's Mountains of Mourne. The climb is Divided Years, possibly the hardest traditional mountain route in the world.*

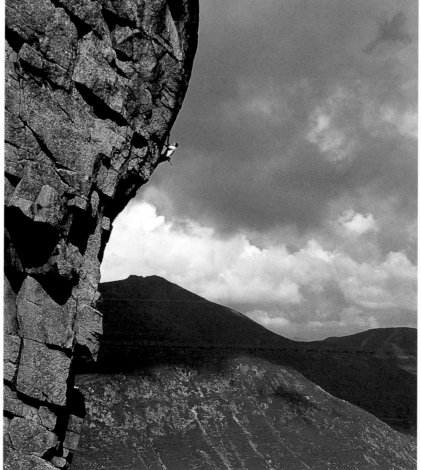

Sea-cliff climbing

The crashing sea adds a very special and satisfying dimension to climbing. It provides a dynamic aspect to what is often a very static pastime. Sea cliffs are serious places. They are often big, under-cut, tidal and intimidating. Your option often is to climb or swim, unless you are prepared to face the embarrassment of the arrival of the lifeboat.

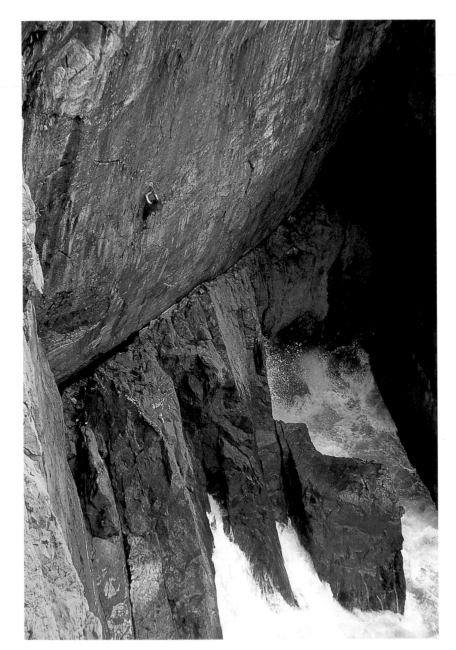

A SPECIAL PLACE WITH SPECIAL PROBLEMS

Never underestimate the sheer power and unpredictability of the sea. The fact that the tide tables are called tidal predictions should provide a good warning. Swell and wave patterns are often influenced by factors thousands of miles away, so perfect weather and a calm sea as you approach your route can be misleading. Tides rush in and take little account of the fact that you are finding the crux unclimbable. As you abseil (rappel) off, you may find that the sun-drenched beach you set off from is now deep ocean. Sea cliffs are not only the home of climbers; most have populations of sea birds in residence during the breeding season. Climbing through their nests can be very disturbing for the birds, but the birds can be very disturbing to you as well. Their defensive skills range from knocking you off your minute holds by dive bombing, through to regurgitating evil-smelling semi-digested fish all over your colourful climbing clothes. The breeding season usually lasts for about six months of the year, leaving plenty of time for you to climb in peace.

VARIABLE ROCK

The rock on sea cliffs varies dramatically from the wave-cleansed lower sections, a joy to behold, to overhanging, shattered blocks covered in lichen and interspersed with grass and mud, guarding your escape at the top. Belays can often be delightfully problematical or non-existent. All this adds to the excitement and satisfaction when you eventually complete your ascent.

◁ *Hard climbing in a very serious setting. A long abseil (rappel) to the start of the route and only one way out.*

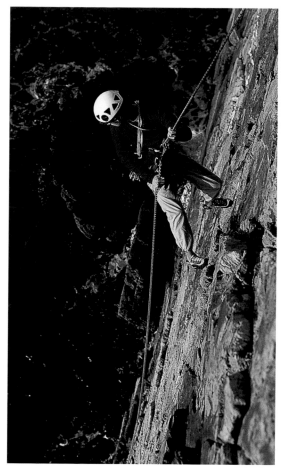

△ *Abseiling (rappelling) down sea cliffs can lead to a difficult escape. It pays to leave a rope in place just in case.*

▷ *Perfect rock, perfect weather – sea cliffs aren't always beasts. Small tidal ranges in the Mediterranean help to create paradise.*

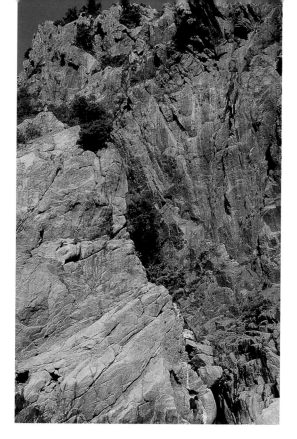

▽ *A classic sea-cliff scene. Not far left to go, but has the climber made other plans for escape should he not be able to make it to the top?*

● **ESCAPING FROM TROUBLE**

If you have to abseil (rappel) down a sea cliff to the start of your intended route, consider carefully the consequences of not being able to finish your climb. Is there an easier route by which you could escape? Is your partner a better climber and able to take over? Is there an easy scramble out of danger? What effect will the tide have on your plan? Is there a problem leaving your belayer on a low stance if you take longer to lead the first pitch? Might they get wet feet – or worse?

Always consider leaving an abseil rope in place, so that you can, as a last resort, prussik back up the cliff.

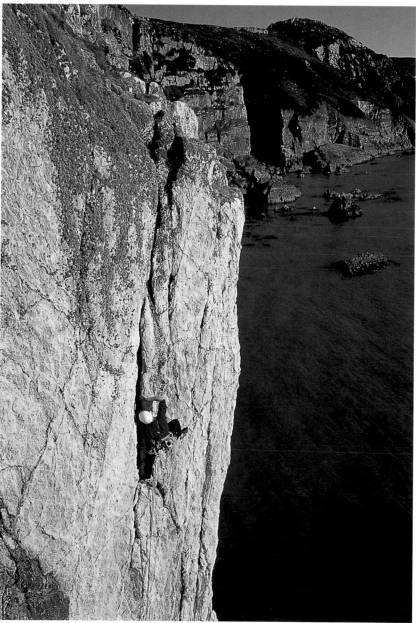

Carrying the gear

The problem of how to carry the gear is one that will have become evident for most climbers who have crossed over from sport to traditional, lead climbing. The amount of gear carried, even for a single pitch climb, is far greater than that carried on a sport route. On multipitch routes this is especially important, particularly if two climbers are alternating leads. Obviously if some of that gear is dropped, it could have serious consequences, not only for the climbers concerned, but others who happen to be below them.

HARNESS OR BANDOLIER (GEAR SLING)
The two choices available are to rack the gear around the harness, which should have adequate facilities, or to use a "bandolier" which is a specially designed padded loop that goes around the shoulders. On steeper routes the bandolier system works very well, and you can simply swap bandoliers at the end of each pitch (at which point it's possible to drop the whole rack). On easier-angled routes, there is a tendency for the bandolier to swing round to the front, making it difficult to see your feet. Using the gear loops on the harness is probably a better option in this situation, and although this may slow you down on the change-overs at the end of each pitch, at least you won't drop the whole rack.

Whichever way, keep the rack organized so everything is in order and always in the same place. Gear will then be quick to retrieve when you're on a long, lonely "run out".

▷ *The system here shows the equipment loops on the harness being used to carry the gear. Many people prefer this method because it allows gear to be arranged so that it is easily accessible.*

▷ *Using a bandolier is a quick and efficient way of carrying gear, especially if two climbers are alternating leads (leading through).*

Problems at the stance

Climbing multipitch routes poses many questions as to what to do and when to do it. If the chosen climb is in an exposed position above a steep slope, a suitable anchor (belay) will be required. Consider the implications of the leader slipping off the first few moves: if they were to land at your feet it shouldn't be a problem. If, however, they were to fall past you and continue down the steep ground, they could pull you after them. This could, at the least, be an inauspicious start to a day's climbing or at worst lead to a very short climbing partnership. Starting a climb from a steep and exposed position is therefore a serious situation, so be aware of potential problems.

If your climb starts from a safe position, it may be okay to stand or sit close to the bottom. There is, however, one complication. If the leader falls with protection placed, they will create a "pulley" effect, lifting the belayer off the ground and possibly into a protruding spike. An upward-pulling anchor becomes much more important here and the biggest problem is making the initial decision to use one, and then a second judgement as to whether it's good enough. A poor anchor may be worse than no anchor because at least you are aware that there is no belay, whereas if you have one that fails – who knows what will happen? Another way around the problem is to place some good protection (running belay) as soon as possible.

▷ Holding a leader fall can be difficult on a multipitch traditional route. The climber (faller) will be climbing past any protection and a fall may result in a greater force being applied to the belayer.

△ Any multipitch climb is complicated if one climber is leading all the pitches. Care is needed at the stances and the rope will have to be run through so that the leader's end is on top of the pile.

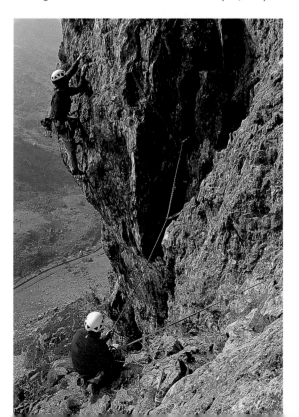

The safety chain

The safety chain includes everything a climber has in terms of equipment and what to do with it. The harness and rope are probably the most important, but the belay device, nuts, hexes, camming devices, slings and karabiners all play their part. The old adage about a chain only being as strong as its weakest link holds good for climbing, too. Always try to be aware of where the weak links in your safety chain might be. The safety chain is present in single pitch climbing (top or bottom roping and leading), but it is at its most complicated and interesting in multipitch climbing situations.

RUNNING BELAYS

The ultimate challenge is perhaps leading your own multipitch route on natural gear (using nuts, hexes and so on) or on bolted protection. When leading, the question of greatest importance for most climbers is, what is the protection (running belays) going to be like?

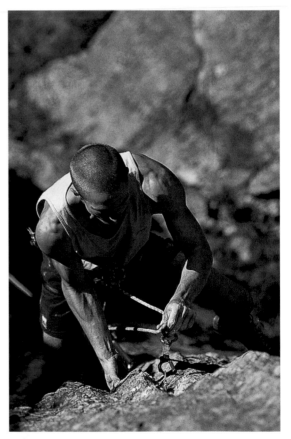

△ *Clipping that all-important running belay. This may have to be done in a physically tiring position.*

◁ *To get good protection for a leader on traditional routes relies on good nuts, cams or slings being placed and, as ever, an alert second as belayer.*

This is a big question and assumes a greater importance on adventure or traditional routes than on a sport route. Protection on traditional routes relies on the placement of nuts, hexes and camming devices, and the leader may find their position precarious while they fiddle a tiny wire behind a small flake of doubtful security. This is a far cry from sport routes where the protection relies on bolts which are usually bombproof and take only seconds to clip. Another consideration is the steeper the route the safer it is (provided your protection does not fail) because it's not the falling off that damages climbers, it's what they hit on their way down, especially if it happens to be the ground which can be pretty unforgiving. If a route is very steep with lots of protection the climber will bounce gently to a stop in mid-air, with the elasticity of the rope absorbing most of the shock. If, on the other hand, the climber slithers down a granite slab, they will feel sore, at the very least. Always get in what you can, when you can; but remember, the more "runners" you place, the more drag you'll get on the rope and more lateral strain, possibly lifting them out.

DYNAMIC ROPES

By the time any climber is contemplating multipitch routes, it should be fairly evident to them that there is a good deal of stretch in any climbing rope and this is a very important factor. Basically this means that any force or shock in the system is absorbed slowly and with less shock to the climber's body or the belay system. If these forces were stopped with a static, or low-stretch rope, there would be considerably more force, not only on the climbers but also on the belay system, with the distinct possibility of failure of part of that system. This is because of the greater force involved or, put more correctly, same amount of force but over a shorter period of time. Apart from the energy absorbed by the rope, energy is also absorbed by the belay plate, the belayer being lifted off the ground, the knots tightening up or, more drastically, a runner failing. Not to be recommended if it's the only

△ **1** On a sport route, clip the bolt with the bent-gate karabiner down and away from you. Now reach down and take the rope between your first and second finger.

△ **2** By hooking the thumb and third finger through the karabiner it will be held steady while the index finger twists the rope into position.

● GETTING IT WRONG

◁ This rope has been clipped the wrong way through the karabiner. If the climber falls there is a distinct possibility that the rope will be taken across the gate and out of the karabiner altogether. Always look ahead to see which way the route is going and clip the quickdraws from behind the gate in the karabiner, with that gate facing away from the direction in which you intend to climb.

one you have got in! The whole safety chain is therefore vital and it is only as strong as its weakest link. However, remember that upward-pulling anchors could, if they are too tight, prevent the belayer from being lifted off the ground, which would possibly weaken the belay. So always, always consider the implications and ask yourself, "What happens if ...?"

Using a single rope

▽ In this situation there will be so much friction created that either the running belays will pull out or the leader will have great difficulty in making further progress.

You have the choice of climbing on one full (single) rope or two half (double) ropes – a full rope is strong enough to use on its own, while a half rope rope must must always be used in conjunction with another half rope (see page 30 on use of double ropes). You need to be aware of the pros and cons of using either, so that you can decide about what is best to use on any given route.

△ Here, the rope is running in a straighter line than in the photograph left. However, the protection could have been extended further with a longer sling.

ROPE DRAG

In many situations climbers use a single rope and this is adequate on either single pitch or easier multipitch routes. There are, however, some limiting factors, which means that in some situations a compromise must be found to deal with a potential problem. Using a single rope on a complicated traditional route can create a lot of friction as the rope passes through the runners. This is called rope drag. On sport routes the bolts are usually in a straight line, so it isn't generally a problem. On traditional routes the protection has to be placed where it occurs and this presents a problem if the rope zigzags from side to side. If the first piece of protection is to the left of the climber

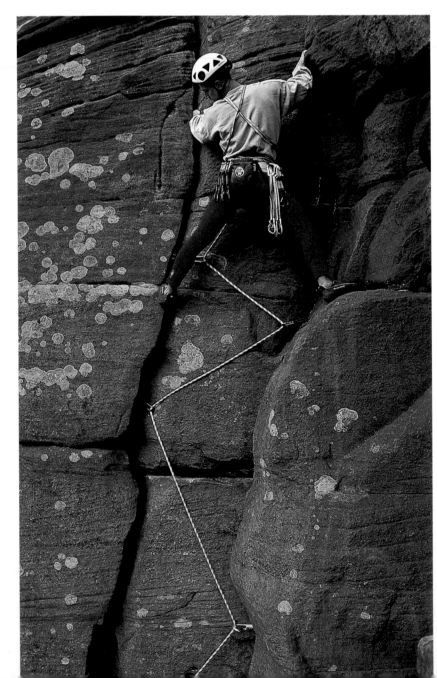

and the second to the right there will be a great deal of friction on the rope, making it difficult to move and causing a severe lateral strain on the runners which could pull them out. Often it's the amount of friction engendered near the top of a pitch rather than at the start that causes the problem, so there is a need to look carefully which way the route goes and extend any runners that are off to one side. The longer the extender, the more likely it is to stay in place. The other answer may be to place the first two runners, then climb down to remove the first one. The other limiting factors with a single rope are the length of abseil (rappel) possible and the difficulty of arranging suitable protection for the second climber on a traverse.

● THE FALL FACTOR

The fall factor refers to the severity of the forces involved in any fall. These forces vary in severity depending on a number of factors. The fall factor is usually expressed as a number, which is arrived at by dividing the length of the fall by the amount of rope that is involved. The numerical values normally run between 0.1 and 2, with 2 creating the greatest impact of force on climber and belayer. For example, if on the third pitch up a multipitch route a leader climbs 3 m (10 ft) above the belay with no runners in between and falls off, they will fall a total of just over 6 m (20 ft) – they will fall below the belay itself. This is a factor 2 fall. The leader has fallen 6 m (20 ft) with 3 m (10 ft) of rope paid out ($6 \div 3 = 2$; $20 \div 10 = 2$). If the same leader falls off at 30 m (100 ft) above the stance with a runner at 27 m (90 ft), they still fall 6 m (20 ft) but the elasticity of a climbing rope and the dynamic factors of the safety chain will absorb most of the force. In this situation the belayer may hardly notice the fall. The fall factor in this situation would only be 0.2, although the actual distance fallen is identical. The moral of this is, get a running belay in as soon as you can after leaving the stance.

△ Multipitch climbing and the fall factor.
A: Fall factor of 2; B: Fall factor of 1; C: Fall factor of 0.5

Rope run out

Length of Fall

Using double ropes

Double ropes are thinner (usually 9 mm) and lighter than single full ropes. This makes them easier to distribute among the climbing party and carry to the crag, mountain or sea cliff. If used properly, they will help reduce or entirely cut out any rope drag. If tied together and used double, they give the potential of a full 50 m (165 ft) abseil (rappel) which can still be retrieved. These advantages are looked at below, and in the following section on abseiling.

TYING ON

This is an easy operation. Simply tie each rope into your harness using the normal figure-of-eight knot re-threaded. It is essential to use two different coloured ropes. This makes life easy when clipping runners. You can let your belayer know that you want slack on red or green or whatever. You should both tie on in the same way and make sure that you have the same coloured rope on the same side (left or right) before setting off on the route.This will help prevent twists in the ropes. Your belayer will thread both ropes through the slots in their belay device. Practice will be needed in paying out separate ropes.

△ It is important to communicate with your belayer when clipping runners to keep them informed as to which rope you need slack on. Keep the instructions short and simple.

ADVANTAGES

Using double ropes can be a tremendous advantage on either harder single pitch or multipitch climbs where the route weaves an intricate path up the crag. Running belays can be clipped either alternately or the ropes can be separated out, one to the left and one to the right. This not only reduces the friction but makes it much easier to arrange protection for the leader and second. Any traverse can be protected for the leader with one rope while the other can be left free to protect the second from directly above. There is also a huge difference in the length of any abseils that can be

▷ Some practice will be needed to overcome the difficulties of handling double ropes, but on longer routes they can be a tremendous advantage.

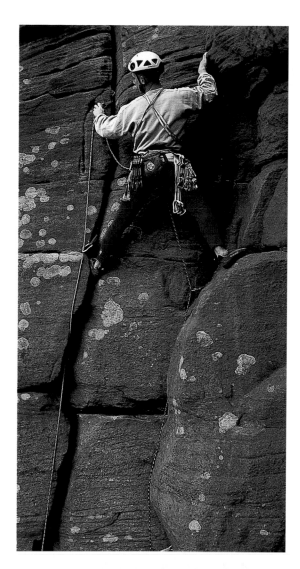

made. A further point is the ease of tying on to two anchor points at the top of the pitch. Simply take one rope to each anchor, tie on with a clove hitch and adjust each independently so both anchors are equally loaded.

TWIN ROPES

Although not particularly popular, this method of ropework has its devotees, particularly where longer multipitch routes are common. The twin rope method uses both ropes as a single rope when climbing. This means putting both ropes through each point of protection, thereby working on the principle that two are better than one. However, long abseils can be made similar to double ropes, so an effective and rapid retreat can be made if necessary. Because of the different thicknesses of all the various ropes involved in climbing, it is essential that they are used only for the purpose they were designed for and that double or twin ropes are not used singly, even for top roping.

◁ *Protecting a climb that has running belays to the left and right of the actual climb is so much easier when double ropes are used, and there is less friction to hinder the leader (see page 28).*

△ *With doubled ropes, any abseil (rappel) can be increased from half the length of the rope to the full length, in most cases from 25 m – 50 m (80 ft – 160 ft).*

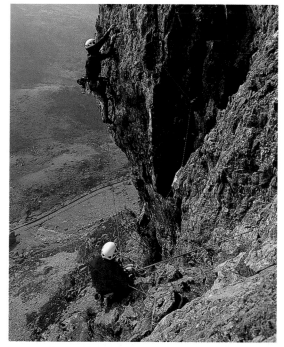

△ *Using doubled ropes in this situation is a real advantage. The leader can arrange better protection for both leader and second.*

● GETTING IT WRONG

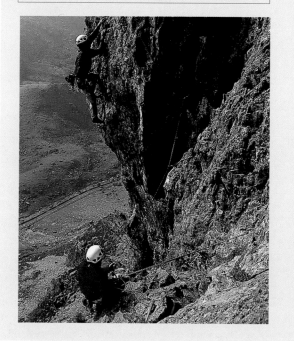

◁ *Although doubled ropes are being used here, it is not to any great advantage. Both ropes are taken in to the corner, which is going to increase friction and give little support to the second climber in the case of a fall.*

Multi-point anchors

▽ Sea cliffs around many coastal areas offer an exciting venue, but the different environment means that specific skills and techniques must be learnt to deal with the hazards of tidal approaches.

On a multipitch route, there are many things to consider when constructing each belay. These will include: the soundness of the anchors; the direction of fall (don't forget that if you are leading through your second will become your leader and will go from climbing below you to climbing above you); your position on the stance; where you will flake the rope (will it be safe from snagging if it simply runs down the rock face?); and how

you will exchange gear when your second arrives at the stance. You will need both hands, so how will you make your second safe while you do this?

DOUBLE ROPES AND ANCHORS

If you are using double ropes, your life is made easier. Where the anchor is a single point and within reach of the belayer, treat both ropes together and tie a clove hitch to the screwgate (locking) karabiner. If there are two anchors, both out of reach, take one rope to each anchor and back to a pear-shaped (HMS) karabiner in the rope loop of the harness and tie with a clove hitch.

By using any of the belay systems described here, any force is transmitted through the belayer and back to the belay, which is a very important point when it comes to dealing with any problems. Any belay anchor or stance will be greatly improved by a good runner being

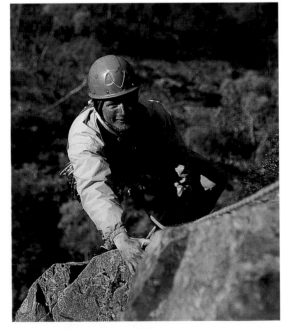

△ The perfect position, high on a route with steep rock which is warm, dry and comforting.

placed immediately on leaving the stance by the leader (see fall factors, page 29). Of particular importance in multipitch climbing is the need to consider whether to belay left- or right-handed. Any belay device should be on the same side as the belay ropes, making it easier to bring the arm back into the locking position; a good deal of dexterity will be required. If the locking hand is on the opposite side of the body while belaying, it will be much more difficult to create the "s" shape through the belay device because the arm cannot be brought back fast enough. This is important on any rock climb but becomes more of a problem when dealing with a tight, constricted or even hanging stance, where there is little or nothing to stand on. All the belayer can do (after tying on of course) is sit back in their harness.

Any multipitch climbing situation is further complicated if one climber is leading all the pitches. In this situation, great care will have to be taken at the change-overs. The ropes will need to be run back through at each stance so that the leader's end is back on top of the pile when they start on the next pitch. If the climbers are leading through this will be unnecessary because each leader's end of rope will be naturally on top of the pile at each stance. On very small or hanging stances the belayer should drape the rope either across the belay ropes or around their feet to make sure it doesn't hang down the rock face and either get jammed in a crack or annoy other climbers. The belayer should always be able to reach the rope to sort any problems out.

● SAFETY CHECKLIST

A good belay will have all of the following:

① Tight ropes leading to two or three strong anchors.
② Equal tension on each rope.
③ The stance will be stable and adjustable from where the belayer stands.
④ Screwgate (locking) karabiners or snaplinks back-to-back on all the anchors.

USING MULTI-POINT ANCHORS WITH A ROPE

△ **1** *Take the rope from your harness to each anchor and back to the harness or rope loop.*

△ **2** *Tie a large overhand knot or a clove hitch to a pear-shaped (HMS) karabiner and clip to your harness.*

USING MULTI-POINT ANCHORS WITH SLINGS

△ **1** *To link two nuts or cams to create a single-point anchor, clip a sling to the karabiner and tie an overhand knot loosely in the sling.*

△ **2** *Clip the other end of the sling to the other karabiner. Adjust the overhand knot to a point where the load is equalized and tighten.*

◁ **3** *Finally, attach the rope to the sling with a karabiner.*

Knots

A concept known as the tool box implies that as you progress in your climbing you will eventually come to possess a lot of alternative techniques that you can use as and when required. You must be clear about when such alternatives might be used and why. The use of knots is a good example. When is it preferable to use the figure-of-eight knot rather than the clove hitch in creating a belay? Which knot is best to use when tying two ropes together to abseil (rappel) off and why?

TYING A BOWLINE KNOT

▷ **1** *Pass a length of rope through the climbing harness, making sure that the manufacturer's instructions are followed closely.*

PROBLEMS WITH THE BOWLINE KNOT

The bowline is commonly used among climbers as an alternative method of tying the rope on to a harness and is perfectly acceptable. However, there are two main considerations that are worth bearing in mind. It is easier to tie the bowline incorrectly than the figure-of-eight. If tied incorrectly, it is dangerous as it converts into a slip knot very easily!

△ **2** *Create a loop in the rope with the main rope on the underside of the loop. Hold firmly with the finger and thumb. Pass the short end of rope through this.*

△ **3** *Then go behind the main rope and back through the loop. Remember, the rope loop should be about fist size when completed.*

△ **4** *Finish with a stopper knot on the inside rope loop: take two turns in reverse around the rope, pass the tail back through the turns and pull tight.*

It is also more difficult to see if the bowline has been correctly tied than the figure-of-eight. This makes it more difficult to check both your own knot simply by casting an eye over it and that of your climbing partner's.

TYING THE BOWLINE

However, it is useful to know how to tie it. Form a loop in the rope about 1 m (3 ft) from the end with the loop to your right (as you look at it) with the main rope underneath the loop. Thread the end of the rope through the harness and then take the end up through the loop, around the main rope and back down through the loop. This has often been quoted as the "rabbit coming out of his burrow, round the tree and back down again". It is vitally important to make sure the end of the rope is on the inside of the knot and finished securely with a "stopper knot" in exactly the same way as the figure-of-eight knot.

ROPE TRICKS

The clove hitch can be tied using only one hand. This may be useful for the leader on arriving at a hanging stance. Having placed a good piece of gear or clipped a bolt, the clove hitch can be tied one-handed, while the other hand keeps you on the rock. The sequence for tying the knot one-handed is shown here.

● KNOTABILITY

The width and construction of your rope will affect how easy (or hard) it will be for you to tie knots in it. Thin ropes tend to be easier to tie knots into than thicker ones. Some ropes are softer and suppler than others, and these qualities also make them easier to handle. Also, a wet and frozen rope might be nearly impossible to tie.

Some rope manufacturers will supply a knotability ratio, designed to give climbers some idea as to how well the rope will handle in this respect. These qualities will also affect how well tied each knot will be.

The Italian hitch can also be tied one-handed using the same technique. However, you take one less twist in the rope before clipping it into the screwgate (locking) karabiner. Double check!

● TYING THE CLOVE HITCH ONE-HANDED

Thumb must point down

△ **1** Clip a karabiner into the belay with the gate towards you and the opening end down. Now take the left-hand rope between finger and thumb.

△ **2** Pull the rope back towards you, twisting the palm of your hand down to form a loop in the rope.

△ **3** Keep the karabiner unlocked up to this stage and complete the hitch by pushing the loop into the karabiner.

△ **4** Finally check the hitch and lock the screwgate (locking) karabiner.

Further knots

The further you venture into the world of multipitch climbing, the more important it becomes to learn to be even more self-reliant and know how to deal with general problems that may crop up. These further knots will add to your armoury and enable you to face new challenges with greater confidence, so that you can get the maximum enjoyment out of the multipitch routes that lie ahead.

△ This chock is threaded on a short length of cord which is then tied with a double fisherman's knot. This is the traditional method of joining two ropes of equal thickness.

TYING A DOUBLE FISHERMAN'S KNOT

△ **1** Take one length of rope back over itself twice and push the end through the hole.

△ **2** Now push the other length of rope through the same hole, but from the opposite direction. Now do exactly what you did with the first length of rope, that is twice round and back through itself.

△ **3** Here, the two completed halves of the knot are being checked. They should be symmetrical and seat well together. If they don't, then try again.

DOUBLE FISHERMAN'S KNOT

The double fisherman's knot has traditionally been used over the years to join two ropes together, often for use in abseiling (rappelling). Although this has now to a certain extent been superseded by the overhand knot, it is still worthwhile knowing how to tie it. The most common use of the double fisherman's knot today is to join the two ends of a short length of rope after threading through nuts and hexes. Take one end of the rope and wrap it twice around itself and then through the hole it has formed. Now push the other end through the loop and wrap this twice around itself and the other rope but in the opposite direction. The two halves of the knot should then slide together and lie side by side. They should look symmetrical. If they are not, then try again. The single fisherman's knot is very similar, almost as strong and uses much less rope. Either will do for joining any two ropes if they are of equal thickness, but be sure to leave adequate lengths of rope after the knot has been tied. The over-hand knot, as mentioned, has to a certain extent supplanted the double fisherman's, particularly when joining ropes together for longer abseils. The reasons will be discussed in greater detail on pages 38–47. Bring the two ends of rope together, form a loop and pass the ends through, allowing at least 1 m (3 ft) of rope on the two trailing ends.

TYING THE FRENCH PRUSSIK (AUTOBLOCK)

The step-by-step sequence below shows how to tie the French prussik and how to rig it for use as a safety back-up to an abseil (rappel). The French prussik is used in other situations as well, mostly for emergency techniques, such as performing assisted and unassisted hoists and escaping from the belay system (see Emergency Ropework for further details).
Advantages: Released under load – amount of friction dependent on turns.
Disadvantages: Can slip without warning. Must be tied with a short sling. Doesn't work with tape (spectra).

TYING THE FRENCH PRUSSIK

△ **1** *The best way of giving protection on any abseil (rappel) if you are the first to go down is to use a French prussik. This is a short loop of 6 mm (¼ in) cord wound four or five times round the abseil rope and attached to the leg loop on the harness. This is slid down the rope with your "bottom" hand as you abseil and should "lock" in an emergency.*

△ **2** *The completed French prussik is shown here.*

△ **3** *The French prussik attached to the leg loop of the harness. This prussik has many more uses (see Emergency Ropework).*

What is abseiling (rappelling)?

▽ Having completed a route, this climber is abseiling (rappelling) back to the ground.

Abseiling (rappelling) is the technique used for descending steep rock either after the climb has been completed, or in certain cases where there is difficult access to the start of the climb. The rope is attached to a safe anchor at the top and a friction device, either a figure-of-eight descender or belay device, placed on the rope and attached to the load-bearing loop of the harness with a screwgate (locking) karabiner. By applying slight pressure with the lower hand below the device, a safe and controlled descent is easily accomplished. Some crags will have abseil descents from the top or in some cases, particularly sea cliffs, an abseil approach. In other situations, such as the onset of bad weather or misjudgement of the difficulty of the route, an abseil may be the only way of getting back down. In the early days of rock climbing, many primitive forms of abseiling were developed. On smaller traditional cliffs it is usually possible to scramble down the easy way. In alpine countries this is not always the case and abseiling is a necessity, particularly on the longer routes. The development of modern equipment makes abseiling far easier than it was but it is important to remember that any abseil is only as safe as the anchor, and that cannot be truly tested until you test it for real.

THE PERFECT POSITION

The perfect position for abseiling is easily achieved on a smooth slab with few ledges or obstructions and it's possible to see all the way down. A high anchor will make life much easier when starting the abseil. This is ideal for a beginner, but with more experience steeper, or even overhanging rock can be descended easily. The anchor must be 100 per cent bombproof. If it isn't, don't abseil! Just as in belaying, there is a live or active hand which is used below the abseil device to control the descent and a dead hand which is usually above the descender, although some beginners will want to use both hands below the device to control their descent at first. Keep the feet shoulder-width

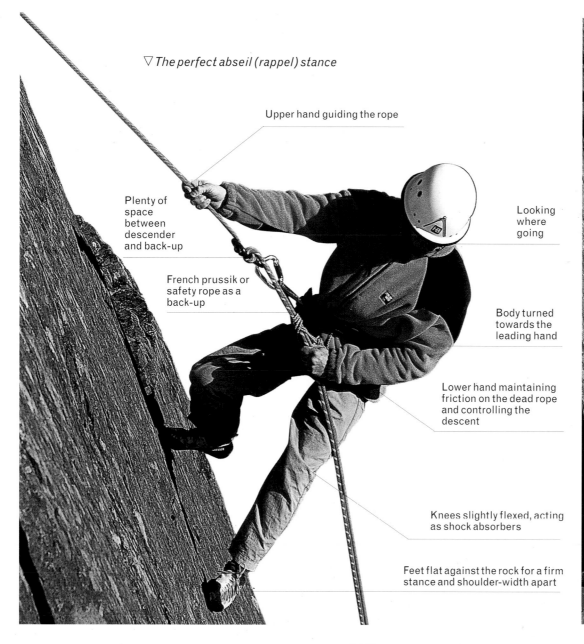

▽ *The perfect abseil (rappel) stance*

Upper hand guiding the rope

Plenty of space between descender and back-up

French prussik or safety rope as a back-up

Looking where going

Body turned towards the leading hand

Lower hand maintaining friction on the dead rope and controlling the descent

Knees slightly flexed, acting as shock absorbers

Feet flat against the rock for a firm stance and shoulder-width apart

apart and turn slightly to the right if right-handed or to the left if left-handed. By turning sideways it becomes much easier to see where you are going and gives more freedom of movement to operate the controlling hand on the descender. The difficult part is committing yourself and going over the edge to start the abseil, but once that is done just feed the rope out and walk backwards down the crag. The feet should be flat against the rock and the closer you are to the horizontal, the less likely your feet are to slip. Flex the knees and control the rope with your bottom hand. There should also be a separate safety rope for beginners or a French prussik (see page 37) as a safety back-up for the more experienced.

△ *This smooth slab is ideal for practising abseiling (rappelling). There are no obstructions or cracks where a boot could get jammed. The ropes can be clearly seen reaching the ground.*

◁ *When beginners practise abseiling (rappelling), there should always be an extra rope used as a safety back-up.*

Abseil (rappel) devices

There are several devices that have been developed especially with abseiling (rappelling) in mind. They give a smooth descent and tend to dissipate the heat generated through friction very well. However, it is worth bearing in mind that most devices designed for belaying can be used for abseiling as well. As a precaution it is a good idea to test a new device in a safe environment (on a short abseil or at an indoor wall) before using it in a more adventurous situation.

THE FIGURE-OF-EIGHT DESCENDER

The figure-of-eight descender is undoubtedly the best device for the job and specifically designed for the purpose, giving a controlled and safe descent. Harnesses which have a central load-bearing loop should present no problems; however, some harnesses require a karabiner to hold the leg loops up or clip the two parts of the harness together. In some cases this can "hold" the karabiner in place and possibly create loading against the gate.

The problem with this type of harness, sometimes referred to as a "Bod" system, is easily overcome by using a "mallion" (designed specifically to take a multi-directional pull) to connect the two parts of the harness together and thus create a central load-bearing loop. It is important to load the rope down through the eye so that it is on top of the descender when it goes over the back bar. If the rope goes up through the "eye" and under the back bar it could catch on a sharp edge of rock and "lock off" around the eye, thus preventing any further descent (see Emergency Ropework).

OTHER ALTERNATIVES

As mentioned, most belay devices offer reasonable options for abseiling and a varying degree of friction on either double or single ropes. The biggest problem with most (Tuber excepted) is a relatively small surface area which doesn't dissipate the heat caused by the friction during the abseil. In a series of long multiple abseils it is important to remove the

▽ *This is a figure-of-eight descender loaded correctly with the rope over the connecting bar. Get into the habit of doing this automatically and always use a screwgate (locking) karabiner.*

▷ *With a "diaper" harness system, it is necessary to connect the two halves of the harness together with a "mallion". This is designed to take a three-way pull – karabiners, even screwgates, are not.*

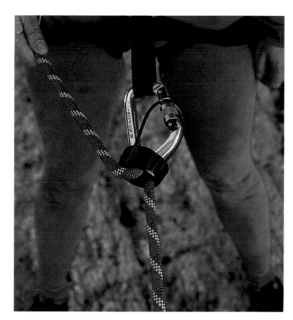

△ This is a belay device which works very well as an abseil device. In a learning or practice situation it is possible to abseil on a single rope.

device quickly at the end of each abseil (rappel). Whichever device is used, it is important to always use either a safety rope or French prussik and clip this to the leg loop below the device with a screwgate (locking) karabiner. This is slid down the rope by the control (lower) hand and if this is removed (for whatever reason) the prussik should automatically lock. Where multiple abseils are involved have a "cow's tail" attachment from your harness to clip the anchor on arrival at the next stance before unclipping from the rope.

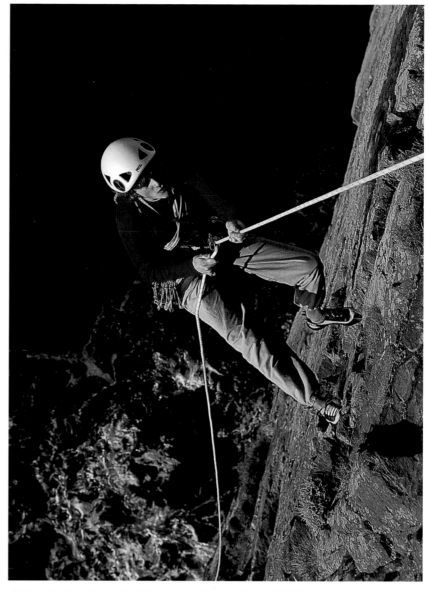

△ Tie a knot in the end of the rope before setting off. This may prevent you sliding off the end!

● GETTING IT WRONG

It is very easy to make mistakes setting up your abseil (rappel). To guard against this, make sure that you check your harness, abseil device and screwgate (locking) karabiner. A common mistake is to feed the rope up through the main hole of the figure-of-eight descender. If the rope is underneath the main bar of the descender it may turn into a "lark's foot" if it catches an edge on the way down. This will lock the descender solid and necessitate a rescue, especially if you are on a free abseil and can't reach the rock.

△ A dangerous situation: the abseil (rappel) device is connected to the harness with a snaplink karabiner.

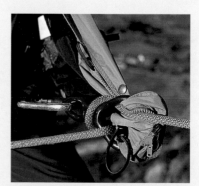

△ The common mistake of allowing clothing to get caught in the descender.

Joining the rope

Traditionally the double fisherman's knot or reef knot with a double fisherman's knot either side have been used to join two ropes, which allows a longer abseil (rappel). A much better method which is becoming common practice is a simple overhand knot. This allows the rope to "roll" outwards away from the rock when it's being retrieved and reduce the chance of the knot jamming on the way down. Always leave a long "tail", roughly 1 m (3 ft), and use a second overhand to prevent clipping the device into the "tails". The second overhand can be removed just before leaving the stance after checking everything (twice). Even when using this method of joining two ropes, it is important to check the position of the knot carefully and

make certain that it will run clear of any cracks. When the first climber has abseiled, get them to try pulling the ropes a little to check whether they will run. If not, try and reposition them. Finally, clip a quickdraw on to the rope that needs to be pulled – just as a reminder.

ABANDONING EQUIPMENT

This is something which no self-respecting climber likes to do, but in serious situations there may be no option. After all, equipment, although it's expensive, can be replaced unlike a life. There are, however, some tricks of the trade which may be of value in the situation where there is a doubtful anchor but with a perfectly reasonable second anchor nearby. Use the doubtful anchor as the main abseil

▽ The overhand knot has recently found favour as a way of joining two ropes. The knot will "roll" away from the rock when the end is pulled and is therefore less likely to jam in a crack.

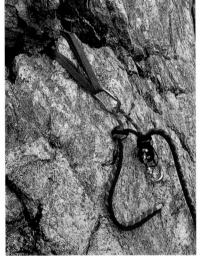

△ This abseil (rappel) has been rigged so that the rope can be retrieved, but not the karabiner and sling. The karabiner is a snaplink, so it may have been better to thread the rope directly into the sling.

▷ A popular way to get down off a crag – but the tree at the top is suffering.

point and put all the load on to that anchor. Now put a good back-up into the second anchor with a few centimetres (inches) of slack in the system and send the heaviest climber first! If the doubtful anchor holds for the heaviest person, in theory the secondary anchor can be retrieved before the second (lighter) person abseils! If nothing else, this should provoke a few arguments among the party as to who is the lightest! It must be stressed that this is for really serious situations only – in particular where equipment is at a premium and may be needed further down the mountain. In 30 years of mountaineering and rock climbing the author has only used the technique three or four times and anyone who tries this must ask themselves what price is equipment anyway.

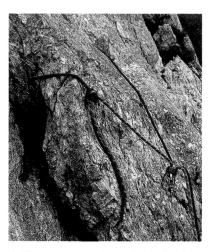

△ The ropes have been joined using an overhand knot and placed over a large flake. There will be some friction when the rope is pulled through once the climber is down.

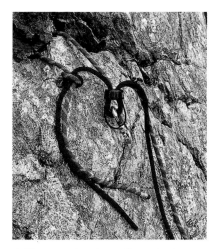

△ The rope has been threaded which may create far too much friction for the rope to be retrieved.

RETRIEVABLE ABSEILING (RAPPELLING)

Do you leave a sling in place to ensure that the rope can be retrieved or do you risk it? In truth there is often no easy solution, unless one person goes down and tries to pull the rope through a few centimetres (inches) first. If at that stage it doesn't run round the anchor, the second person would have to rearrange the rope and try again. As a general rule, if there is any doubt leave a sling. On long multipitch routes many leaders carry a few metres (feet) of cord or tape specifically for rigging abseils and leaving behind, and a penknife for cutting to the required length. It is worth being particularly careful when dealing with a rounded spike – there is a tendency for rope to "roll" off when the rope is loaded. In this situation, a short length of tape would be much less likely to roll.

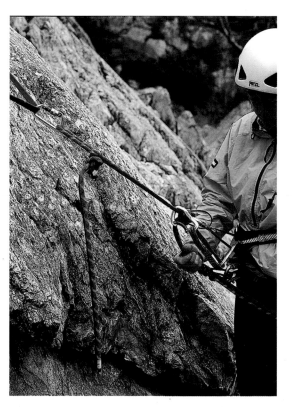

◁ The perfect retrievable abseil (rappel). However, the screwgate (locking) karabiner and sling will be left behind. The climber has a French prussik for safety and has clipped a quickdraw to the rope that will need to be pulled through once down.

● ABSEILING (RAPPELLING) IN SAFETY – TOP TIPS

- Make sure your ropes reach the ground, or at least to another stance.
- Get a sound anchor, at any price.
- Practise and become familiar with the technique.
- Use a French prussik from your leg loop, and of the right length. This is usually a 1.25 m (4 ft) length of 6 mm (¼ in) cord joined with a double fisherman's knot.
- Keep your anchor as high as possible in relation to the take-off point.
- Don't use trees unless you really have to, and then leave a sling or length of tape.
- Back the anchor up if in doubt.
- Buy yourself a mallion if your harness requires "holding" together at the front, for example a "Bod" system.

The anchor point

On sport crags, the anchor points are invariably good, although don't trust bolts implicitly, especially some of the ancient relics from a bygone age and always abseil (rappel) with care. The steadier you go down, the less strain there will be on the anchor, ropes and harnesses. On traditional climbing areas it can be much more difficult and the perfect anchor, one which allows the rope to be retrieved, is often elusive. In some cases it may be necessary to abandon a sling and abseil off this rather than risk getting the rope jammed in a crack. Trees often make excellent anchors but this causes serious damage when ropes are pulled down. However, if it is absolutely necessary, leave a sling in place and abseil off this rather than placing the rope directly round the tree. Many trees have been killed over the years by continual use, particularly by people abseiling at many climbing venues throughout the world. This is bad enough, but further damage will be caused to the crag when the root systems die, so use them only as a last resort. Choose a high anchor point, at least above waist-height. Having a low anchor not only raises the risk of the rope slipping off but increases strain on the anchor because of the outward directional pull on it. Finally a low anchor will make life difficult, and therefore dangerous, when you are going over the edge. Last but by no means least, choose the place to abseil with care, making sure that no one is climbing up and giving a good warning shout of "rope below" when throwing the ropes down just in case.

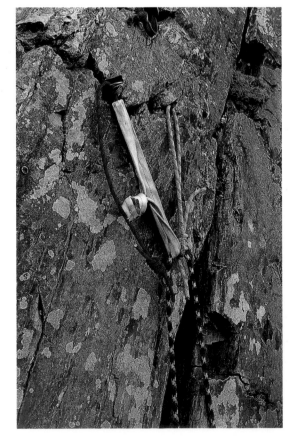

◁ *Where there are several pieces of equipment to abseil (rappel) off, try and link all the anchors to ensure all are equally loaded and independently tied off.*

▷ *A well-placed nut will save the situation should the anchor fail. Note that the nut is not loaded – it is a back-up. If all has gone well, the last person to abseil (rappel) may risk removing it.*

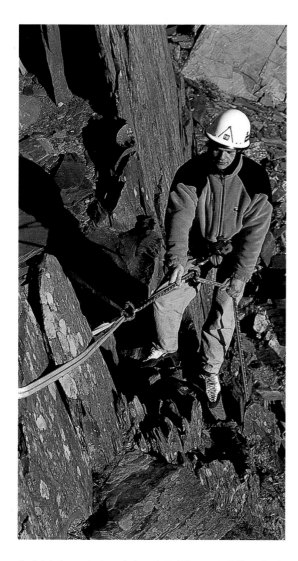

△ *A high anchor point makes life easy at the start of an abseil (rappel). The anchor is above the belay device and allows the abseiler to get the correct position before going over the edge.*

The popularity of abseiling as the normal means of descent from many crags is due to the dislike of slithering down muddy paths in expensive footwear that is totally unsuited for the purpose. Abseiling is an essential (and inherently dangerous) technique to be learnt. There are many shiny gadgets on the market which are designed to make life easier, but none are of the slightest use unless the anchor point is chosen with care and due regard for the consequences of the abseil. Once you have leant back and weighted the rope and anchor, there is no turning back. The anchor must not fail! When abseiling, all climbers trust the rope without question, but remember the rope is only as good as the anchor.

● GETTING IT WRONG

A very poor site has been chosen, especially for someone who is just learning. The abseiler will be unable to see if the ropes reach the bottom because of the extremely steep take-off point and low anchor. This will create difficulties as they go over the edge. They could turn upside down because of the direction of pull on the anchor. There have been a few cases where a hole has been punched in the karabiner gate, causing the system to fail. This is much more likely if an anchor point which is lower than the take-off point has been chosen, allowing the descender to flick over and pull across the gate.

△ *Choice of anchors for an abseil (rappel) is crucial for success. Here the anchors are too low.*

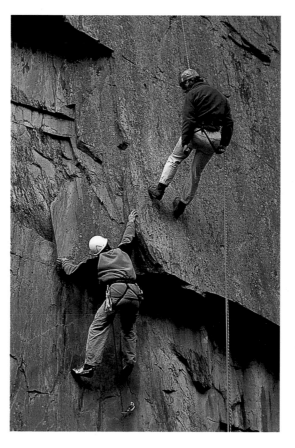

◁ *Never abseil (rappel) above a climber who may be leading a route. The last thing a leader wants is for someone to dislodge stones on to their head.*

Security

There are several ways in which you can make abseiling (rappelling) a safer activity. You can even abseil if you drop your belay device – using the Italian hitch.

THE ITALIAN HITCH

Although the Italian hitch is not ideal for abseiling it can be used in a situation where no other device is available, although in double ropes extensive twisting will occur. If the rope is used singly (that is, tied off at one end) the Italian hitch is much easier to use, although it still may twist alarmingly. It is essential to use a large pear-shaped (HMS) screwgate (locking) karabiner (not a twistlock type) to ensure the rope runs smoothly and to increase the heat dissipation. To create an Italian hitch, form two loops, right over left, right over left, fold the loops together and then clip the two ropes into the karabiner. The use of a French prussik as a "back-up" will make it possible to untangle the ropes. In spite of the problems, this method can be used in any situation where the abseil device has been dropped or forgotten. If using this method, ensure that the Italian hitch is operating against the back bar of the karabiner and not anywhere near the gate.

USING A PRUSSIK

This is a length of 6 mm (¼ in) cord about 1.5 m (4½ ft) long. Tie the ends together with a double fisherman's knot to form a loop; the loop should run from the thumb to a point level with the elbow. This is wound at least four or five times round the ropes, taking care to include both ropes if double ropes are being used.

Keep the French prussik short and snug and do not use any other prussik knots in this situation as they are not easily released once they are loaded.

Consider also how each device will be affected if the prussik is too long. In some cases the prussik will simply be released and in others it may be dragged into the abseil device.

△ **1** If you want to stop mid-descent (to retrieve some gear left on a route, for example), you can use the following method to free your hands.

△ **2** Take a length of rope around your leg for three or four turns. Make sure you keep hold of the controlling rope.

△ **3** Now carefully let go of the controlling rope. The wraps around your thigh should stop your descent. Your hands are now free.

Either way it could be disastrous and best not to find out, so keep those prussiks short and snug. There are, of course, some devices that are designed to lock automatically, so a French prussik may be unnecessary, unless of course a malfunction (grit, dirt or inexperience) causes a problem in any way. In that case you'll look foolish if you haven't used one. An alternative way of providing safety back-up once the first person is down (or there is a responsible person already at the bottom) is to get them to pull gently on the bottom end of the rope. This should have the effect of locking off the abseil device and will not only give confidence to beginners but could save a good deal of time if multiple abseils are involved.

● SECURITY FROM BELOW

Today this is the standard way of helping beginners to gain confidence when learning to abseil (rappel). Good communication is important for both parties. Surprisingly little tension is required on the rope and with a little practice the person at the bottom can lower the abseiler (rappeller) a few centimetres (inches) and then lock off again. The same technique can also be used in a situation where a series of abseils is needed to get off a major climb. The first climber should go down protecting themselves with a French prussik and the second climber protected by the first in exactly the same way. This will speed the whole process up for both parties. If the abseil is an emergency one where the Italian hitch is used, the technique will still work although in some cases there will be a little less friction on the rope so more tension will be needed. The amount of tension needed will depend on the amount of friction, and this will depend upon several factors: the thickness of the ropes, whether you are using single or double ropes, the type of belay device, the weight of the abseiler, and so on.

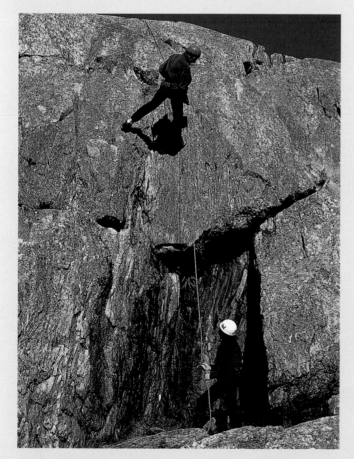

△ **1** *An alternative method of providing security for the abseiler (rappeller): the first abseiler down simply holds the abseil rope lightly.*

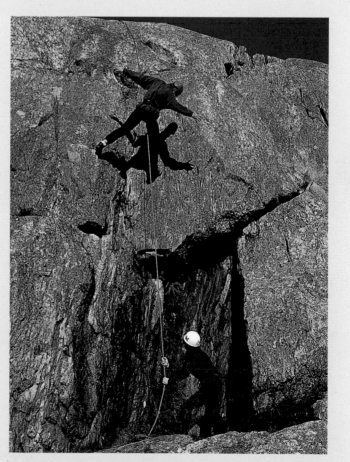

△ **2** *Should they need to stop the next abseiler from descending any further, they simply pull on the rope, applying tension to the system. This will lock the abseil device.*

Getting out of trouble

By following basic, standard procedures and the advanced techniques taught in this book, many potentially dangerous situations can be easily solved. The ropework methods have been taught for the very good reason that, should any problem arise, there will be a simple answer to deal with it. All the different skills involved in rescue can be learnt individually and then used as needed. Treat each situation as the occasion demands – look at the problem, don't rush and, above all, think clearly and decide what to do and when. If in doubt, get help.

LOCKING OFF A BELAY DEVICE

Locking off a belay device under load is the action to take in most incidents. It allows a breathing space and ensures nothing else can go wrong. Moreover, it leaves the belayer with both hands free. The belayer can either lower the casualty or hoist them to the stance, whichever is most appropriate. Always make sure that the rope is tied off against the back bar of the karabiner and not the gate.

△ **1** *Keeping the rope in the "locked" position – take a bight of rope through the karabiner.*

△ **2** *Take a second loop through the first loop and pull the rope tight.*

△ **3** *Now tie a couple of half-hitches back around the karabiner.*

● GETTING IT WRONG

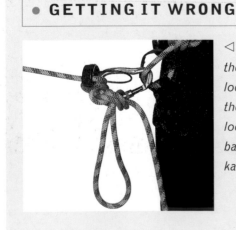

◁ *In this picture the rope has been locked off against the gate. Always lock off against the back bar of the karabiner.*

△ **4** *The belay device is now locked off and you can take both hands off the rope.*

△ **5** *To release the load take the half-hitches out and pull the tail, keeping the hand against the rope and the belay device.*

Prussik knots

Prussik knots consist of a 6 mm (¼ in) cord which is wound several times round the main climbing rope, tied and then locked off. All prussik knots have slightly different properties and it is important to be aware of them. For example, the French prussik (see page 37) can release under load. Therefore there are situations where the French prussik can be dangerous when climbing (prussiking) up a rope. If the French prussik is grabbed in the heat of the moment it could let you down.

THE ORIGINAL PRUSSIK
Advantages: Quick, easy to tie one-handed. Number of turns can be increased when using thicker ropes or to increase the amount of friction.
Disadvantages: Tendency to jam solid especially on wet ropes. Not recommended with tape (spectra) – cannot be released under load.

△ **1** *Take the prussik loop two or three times around the main rope and push the end through itself. Pull tight.*

△ **2** *The completed knot. It should be neat and tidy if it is to work efficiently on the rope.*

THE KLEMHEIST
Advantages: Any thickness of rope can be used – the number of turns is variable. It can be tied either with tape (spectra).
Disadvantages – Cannot be released easily when it is loaded.

△ **1** *Take the prussik loop three or four times around the main rope and push the lower end through the top end.*

△ **2** *The completed Klemheist. It can now be clipped directly on to the waist harness with a screwgate (locking) karabiner.*

● SPECIALIZED EQUIPMENT

Mechanical devices can be used instead of prussik knots; they do the job more efficiently but are relatively expensive. If rock climbing is to be attempted in serious situations, either in sea cliff or high mountain locations, their use may be worth considering. Ascenders, metal clamps which attach to the rope, come in a variety of guises, with or without handles, and will slide one way (preferably upwards) and, by means of a cam, lock on the rope when downward pressure is applied. All are supplied with manufacturer's instructions which must be followed to the letter.

△ *The handled ascender (left) and ropeman have almost rendered prussik loops obsolete but are relatively expensive pieces of equipment for occasional use.*

Hoisting

There are situations in which you may need to help your second over a difficult move by giving them a quick hoist on the rope. Or you may need to help a climber knocked unconscious by a falling stone. These are but two of the many, though hopefully rare, situations in which you may need to set up a hoist. There are two basic kinds of hoist.

ASSISTED HOIST

This is a relatively simple method of giving someone a quick pull over a difficult move. Even so, it should only be tried when all other efforts have failed. The stages are:

① Lock off the belay device as described on page 48.
② Attach a French prussik or auto-block (see page 37) to the rope immediately below the belay device and clip with a screwgate (locking) karabiner to the rope loop around the harness, making sure there are a few centimetres (inches) of slack in the prussik. If there is more the hoist will be inefficient.
③ Throw a loop of rope down to the second instructing them to clip it to the main load-bearing loop of their harness with a screwgate karabiner. The rope now goes from their harness, through the French prussik and belay device, back down to their harness and back up to you. Untie the belay device carefully, making sure the French prussik is gripping the main rope.
④ Get the second to pull on the rope running down to them while you pull on the rope coming back up.

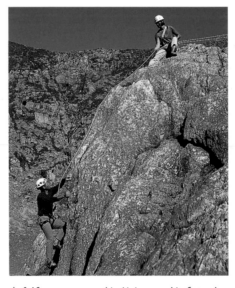

△ **1** *If your second is tiring and is faced with a difficult move, you can perform an assisted hoist. First, lock off the belay plate.*

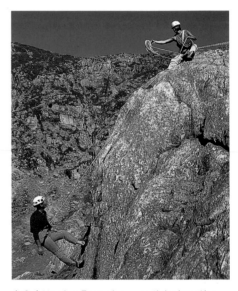

△ **2** *Attach a French prussik below the plate and around the main climbing rope. Clip with a screwgate (locking) karabiner to the rope loop in your harness.*

△ **3** *Throw a loop of rope to your second so they can clip it to a load-bearing part of the harness with a screwgate. Untie the locked-off belay device and check that the French prussik is holding.*

△ **4** *Your second can then pull on the loop running down to them while you pull on the rope coming back up. Keep an eye on the French prussik; they can let you down.*

MECHANICAL ADVANTAGE

In technical terms the assisted hoist gives a 3:1 mechanical advantage, and the advantage of both climbers pulling on the ropes. The French prussik gives a one-way braking system, so the leader and second can take a rest. Watch the prussik closely. If it is too tight it will jam in the system and if it is too loose it won't grip the main rope. In theory, the assisted hoist can be used where the second is less than 15 m (50 ft) below the leader, although in practice it can be difficult to get the rope in position and communicate effectively at this distance. When the system is established there are three lengths of rope between both climbers – and there is generally only 50 m (165 ft) available. If the climbers are more than 15 m (50 ft) apart, can't communicate or have difficulty in getting the rope in position, the unassisted hoist must be used.

UNASSISTED HOIST

The unassisted hoist would be used if you did not have enough rope to send down to the climber who needs a hoist. It would also be used if the climber in question could not assist you in any way (they are unconscious or have received an injury to the arm, for example). Be warned: this is a very tiring exercise to undertake, and you may find it easier to lower rather than to hoist.

① Lock off the belay device and attach the French prussik (or autoblock) as in the assisted hoist.
② Tie a further prussik on the main rope. Attach the loop of rope (which in the assisted hoist would have gone to the second climber) via two snaplink (back-to-back) or screwgate (locking) karabiners. This will give a greater radius for the rope to run round and reduce the friction.
③ Slide the second prussik down the rope as far as possible with the foot. Now untie the locked-off belay plate, again ensuring the prussik is working effectively and pull on the tail.

The Z system, or 3:1 ratio, is exactly the same as before but over a much shorter distance, so the autoblock (brake) will be needed after each pull while the lower prussik is pushed down ready for the next hoist. Always keep hold of the "tail" of the loop and keep a watchful eye on both prussiks.

△ **1** *Lock off the belay device and attach the French prussik (or autoblock) to the rope loop around the harness.*

△ **2** *Place the second prussik around the main climbing rope and clip in a loop with either a screwgate (locking) karabiner or two snaplinks to increase the radius and decrease the friction.*

△ **3** *Slide the second prussik down the rope with your foot until you can make an effective pull. The procedure may have to be repeated several times because the casualty can only be moved a short distance at a time.*

Escaping the system

Y ou may need to get out of the belay and free yourself from the rope to go and get help in the event of an accident or abseil (rappel) down to your partner to render first aid. This is a serious situation, especially if the injured climber is hanging by their harness in free space and is unconscious. This is a worst case scenario, for in this situation you will have to act very quickly to prevent them from suffocating as they hang backwards.

ANCHOR WITHIN REACH
The use of the Italian hitch in this situation should allow you to either lower the casulty or set up a 3:1 hoist to pull them up to the stance, once their injuries have been dealt with. When you have escaped the system, you can either abseil (rappel) or prussik to your casualty, or get help.

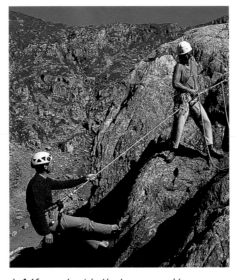

△ **1** *If you decide that you need to escape the system, first stabilize the weight of the climber on the end of the rope.*

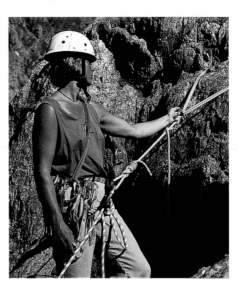

△ **2** *Lock off the belay plate and confirm that you can reach the anchor by touching it.*

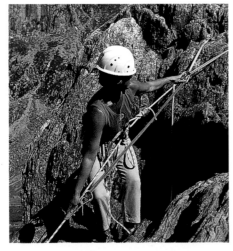

△ **3** *Now put a French prussik just below the belay device and attach this to the anchor with a sling and screwgate (locking) karabiners, and weight this.*

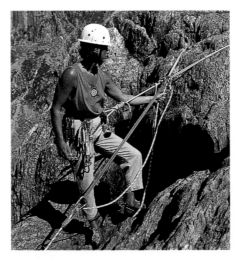

△ **4** *Take the main rope, released from tension by the prussik and sling, and attach this to the anchor via an Italian hitch that is tied off to a screwgate (locking) karabiner.*

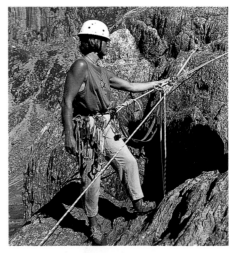

△ **5** *Release the French prussik and remove it. The weight will now be off your harness. Retrieve any gear not needed. Protect yourself with a cow's tail and escape from the system.*

ANCHOR OUT OF REACH

If the anchor point is out of reach, proceed as with the anchor in reach, but taking several extra steps as shown in the sequence here. If you are working with a single anchor point, it should be possible to transfer everything to the main anchor point and retrieve the rope. Otherwise, with one end of rope trapped in the system, you may have to prussik down the loaded rope to reach the casualty – unless, of course, you have some spare rope with you.

▷ **1** *Lock off the belay device and tie a French prussik on the load rope. Tie a Klemheist prussik with a tape sling around the main belay rope. Attach a screwgate (locking) karabiner and connect the two prussiks with a sling.*

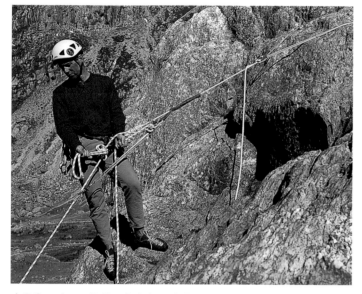

△ **2** *Create an Italian hitch and clip this to the Klemheist with a separate screwgate karabiner. Release the belay plate (gently) and pull the spare rope through the Italian hitch.*

△ **3** *Lock off the Italian hitch in the Klemheist and make yourself safe with a cow's tail. You can now untie and escape the system. Leave a knot in the end of the rope, just in front of the Klemheist.*

△ **4** *Take the rope back to the main anchor and use a tied-off Italian hitch to secure it. Don't hesitate to back up the main anchor if there is any doubt.*

△ **5** *Both prussiks can now be released so the load is transferred to the Italian hitch on the main anchor. Where there are several belay points, tie a Klemheist around all the ropes.*

Accompanied abseil (rappel)

▽ *An accompanied abseil (rappel) in action. This can be a particularly useful technique where either minor injuries are concerned or the casualty is nervous of abseiling.*

This is not as difficult as it sounds and can be used to introduce beginners who are simply nervous of abseiling, or in situations where there is an injured person to assist down the crag. Accompanied abseils can be done on either single or double ropes but due consideration must be given to the combined weight of two people on the abseil device and extra friction may be required.

HOW TO GO ABOUT IT

Tie an overhand knot in the middle of a long 2.5 m (8 ft) sling and clip the abseil (rappel) device via a screwgate (locking) karabiner into both halves of the sling. One end of the sling is for each abseiler and the control rope is taken by the person in charge of the abseil. A French prussik on the leg loop is essential and if extra friction is required use an Italian hitch on the load-bearing loop of the harness. The position of the casualty can be adjusted by changing the position of the overhand knot in the sling. If the knot is in the middle they will be alongside. If the knot is moved 50–70 mm (2–2¾ in) one way with the controller on the longer end the casualty will be above (across the lap) of the controller. On steeper ground it should be possible to straddle the casualty and put them face outwards, which is particularly useful if they have sustained a lower leg injury. A quickdraw clipped between the load-bearing loops on the harnesses should ensure the casualty's back is clear of the rock. It is worth noting that a close eye can be kept on the casualty when using this method, which is a distinct advantage.

ABSEILING (RAPPELLING) PAST A KNOT

If it is known there is a knot or damaged area within the rope, attach a French prussik above the abseil device, ensuring that it stays within reach (you can use a quickdraw). Three hand-widths above the knot, lock the French prussik off and apply a second abseil device or Italian hitch to the harness and lock off before removing the first one. By releasing the French prussik it should be possible to continue with the abseil. Before you do so, make sure that you reposition the French prussik on the leg loop.

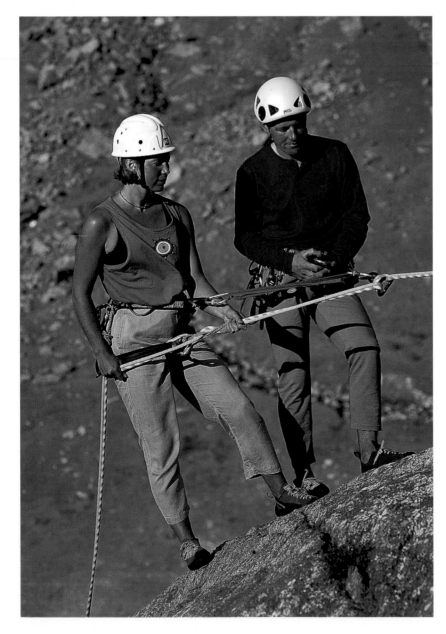

LOWERING PAST THE KNOT

For whatever reason you need to lower your partner off a crag, you can combine the length of two ropes tied together to get maximum distance. It will entail lowering past a knot. Equally, if your rope has been damaged and you want to lower someone, you will have a knot to pass. Tie a simple overhand knot at the damaged area, thus eliminating it. Lower the casualty until the knot is three hand-widths from the lowering device and apply a French prussik with a 1.2 m (4 ft) sling to the anchor. Thread a second lowering device or Italian hitch, locked off above the knot. Remove the first lowering device and release the French prussik temporarily to allow the knot to pass through. Then continue lowering.

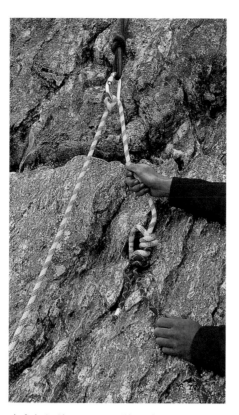

△ **1** *Join the ropes with either a double fisherman's or an overhand knot. Lower the casualty down until the second rope, which is already tied on, appears.*

△ **2** *Apply a French prussik, using a 1.2 m (4 ft) sling to allow sufficient freedom of movement and lock the lowering device off.*

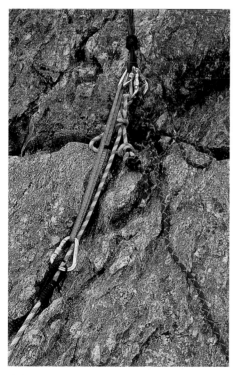

△ **3** *Thread a second lowering device or Italian hitch on to the second rope above the knot and lock this off.*

△ **4** *The first device can now be removed. This will introduce a little slack into the system but if the French prussik is released slowly the weight will eventually come on the second device.*

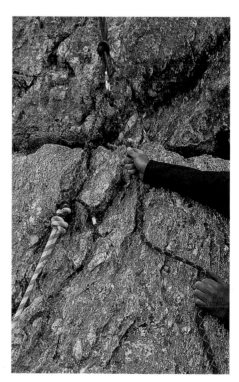

△ **5** *Remove the French prussik temporarily to allow the knot to go through the system and continue lowering as before.*

Dealing with traverses

raverses present the leader with a variety of problems. They not only have to protect themselves, but they should also be thinking about how best to protect their second when they come to climb the pitch. If something goes wrong while the second is on the traverse, then these problems become considerable. For example, if a second is unable to make the moves on a straight up and down pitch, or is injured, then the leader can arrange to hoist them over the difficult move (see page 50) or right up to their stance if necessary. But in the case of a traverse the leader's belay is not directly above the second. A hoist becomes much more problematic. However, there are solutions.

● THE STAGES OF TRAVERSE RESCUE

These diagrams clearly show the main stages in performing a traverse rescue.

A–Leader's harness

B–Anchors

C–Clove hitch

D–Second's harness

① Belay device locked off with two half hitches

② French prussik

③ Loop from belay end of rope

△ **1** *Tie the belay plate off and apply a French prussik to the load rope. Now take a loop of rope from the belay end, that is direct from the anchor, and throw it to the casualty.*

⑤ Italian hitch

⑥ Pull here to bring casualty across

④ Screwgate clipped to loop in belt

△ **2** *Instruct the casualty to clip this to the main load-bearing loop of the harness with a screwgate (locking) karabiner. The other end goes to an Italian hitch on the main anchor.*

⑧ Release French prussik

⑨ Release belay device slowly

⑦ Lock off Italian hitch

△ **3** *Pull the loop as far as possible then lock off the Italian hitch. Now release the French prussik, allowing the tension in the rope loop to swing the casualty across.*

EMERGENCY ROPEWORK

their harness. Do not use the rope loop on the harness in this case. Create an Italian hitch in the rope that is running back to the belay and attach to the main anchor. The casualty can pull on the loop going towards them while the belayer pulls on the loop and ties off the Italian hitch when no more of the loop can be pulled in. The next step is to release the French prussik on the belay plate slowly so the tension in the loop swings the casualty towards the belayer. Lock off the belay plate and repeat the procedure, pulling on the loop, to bring the casualty to a point alongside or just below the belay.

△ *Any route that contains a traverse can present both the leader and second with a problem. If a climber falls off while either above or below their partner it can be fairly easy to sort things out. If however the climber falls off on a traverse the situation will require a little more cunning.*

THE STAGES

Lock off the belay plate and apply a French prussik immediately behind the plate. If the casualty is relatively close, a couple of slings tied together is the answer. Simply throw one end and pull them aboard. It may be necessary to release the belay device a little and give enough slack rope for them to reach the stance. If the casualty is 7–10 m (20–30 ft) away, lock the plate off and apply a French prussik as above, and throw them a loop from the belay end of rope so the rope is going from the anchor to the casualty and back to the belayer. Make sure there are no twists in this loop and get them to clip this to the load-bearing loop on

IN EXTREMES

In extreme cases where a loop will not reach the casualty, it may be necessary to escape the system and throw the end of rope to them and then proceed. A lateral strain will be applied to any running belays and, if they fail, the casualty could pendulum rapidly towards the anchor. Once the casualty is pulled in, the original end to which they were attached can be untied, the rope retrieved and an abseil (rappel) retreat undertaken.

PRUSSIKING UP A ROPE

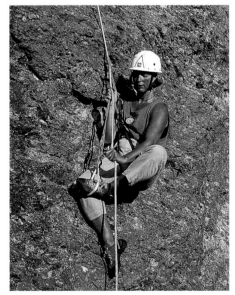

△ **1** *Two prussiks are used to ascend the rope, one tied above the other. You can use Klemheist or original prussiks. The top one is connected to the harness and the bottom one, via a sling, to the foot.*

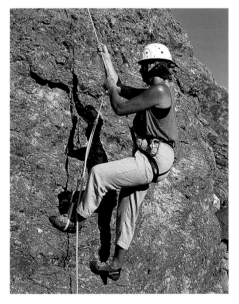

△ **2** *Sit back in your harness and weight the prussik connected to your waist. Move the foot prussik up the rope.*

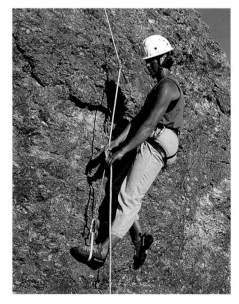

△ **3** *Now weight the foot prussik by standing in it. Move the freed waist prussik up the rope and weight that in turn. Repeat the procedure to the top.*

2

FURTHER SKILLS

The art of getting out of trouble is not to get into it in the first place. But all experienced rock climbers will agree that even the best-laid plans can go wrong and problems have a nasty habit of appearing when they are least expected. As you venture further afield, into the mountains and other remote areas, you will inevitably be called upon for more than just your climbing skills. Knowing first aid, having the ability to navigate through unfamiliar terrain, and being able to read mountain weather are all skills that will serve to make you a better and more competent, all-round rock climber. The more skills you possess the better equipped you will be to deal with problem situations effectively.

Opposite: *The full outdoor experience – wilderness, solitude and a sense of self-reliance. Rock climbing in this environment requires more skill and judgement than that required on a roadside crag or indoor climbing wall.*

Emergency procedures

The mountains are neither for nor against a climbing team, so they are not out to get you. From time to time, however, climbers' interaction with the mountain can lead to an accident or injury. This can be caused by you hitting the mountain, by some of the mountain hitting you, or by the weather turning against you. If this happens, you can load the odds in your favour by knowing how to deal with an incident and how to preserve life.

FIRST AID

In the event of an accident, stop, think – think again. Then act decisively. This is more easily said than done. A lot will depend on your own experience with first aid. It is strongly recommended that you attend one of the many first-aid courses to acquaint yourself with some of the basic knowledge for dealing with an accident victim.

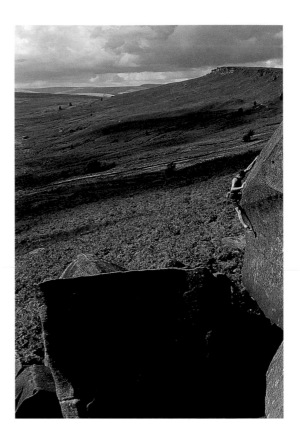

△ Carefree and fun but let's hope your friends can cope if the holds run out.

◁ A good knowledge of how to deal with emergencies is vital in wild, isolated country.

● THE FIRST PRINCIPLES AND AIMS OF FIRST AID

① Your own safety is paramount – you are not only useless if you become a victim as well, you will also complicate the situation and put everyone at greater risk.

② Leave the patient no worse off than when you began. Only move an injured person if it is absolutely essential. Often the best first aid is to do nothing.

③ Reassure the patient. This will contribute to a feeling of well-being and will help fight medical shock.

④ Keep the patient warm. A major job in a mountain setting.

The aims of first aid:
• preserve life
• prevent deterioration
• promote recovery

You should arrange for help to be mobilized, and continue with the aims of first aid until the arrival of medical aid, which will most commonly be in the form of the Mountain Rescue team.

● VITAL SIGNS

Before you can tell whether someone is injured or ill, you must know the vital signs of a normal, healthy adult.

• Breathing – 10 to 15 breaths per minute. This will obviously be increased if they have just run up a hill or fallen off the crux of a climb.

• Pulse – 60 to 80 beats per minute. Again, this may be much higher if they have been through a traumatic experience or heavy exertion.

• Level of consciousness:
Alert – capable of initiating a coherent conversation
Vocal – may speak if spoken to, but incoherently

Responsive – responding to pain
Unresponsive – not responding to pain

The important thing for the first aider is to monitor whether the patient is remaining stable or becoming more or less conscious. Do this by recording breathing and pulse rate and level of response, every 10 minutes.

Colour – pink and oxygenated. The inside of the lips is the best place to check this, as it avoids confusion due to outside factors and difference in skin colour.

Temperature – core temperature of 37.5°C (98.6°F). Difficult to determine in the mountains with no equipment.

◁ *Monitoring an injured person's vital signs is one of the main responsibilities of the first aider once you have stabilized the situation.*

Dealing with an accident

An accident in a crag setting will unnerve you, so you must be sure to assess the situation accurately before acting. Establish whether the victim is conscious by introducing yourself and if necessary by gently squeezing the shoulders. Then carry out the A B C of survival:

A – AIRWAY. Check they have an airway that is open; if not open it. If someone is speaking or screaming their airway is open.

B – BREATHING. Check by looking, feeling and listening.

C – CIRCULATION. Do they have a pulse? Check the neck pulse for 15 seconds. Check for severe bleeding.

UNCONSCIOUSNESS

A person is unconscious if they cannot instigate a coherent conversation. One in four unconscious persons will die if they are left lying on their backs. They must be placed in the recovery (safe airway) position and monitored for A B C.

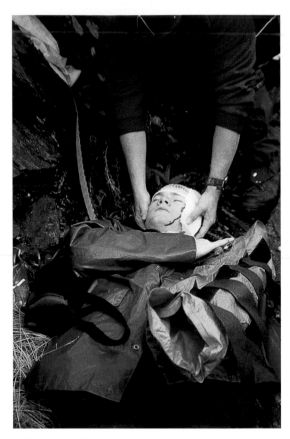

△ Dealing with bleeding – use direct pressure, elevation and then good padding and bandaging.

SHOCK

Medical shock is the reaction of the body to insufficient oxygen reaching the vital organs due to a drop in the effective circulating blood volume. The signs of shock are:

• a rapid weak pulse
• rapid breathing
• cold, pale, clammy skin and a feeling of anxiety

You are dealing with a life-threatening condition. Treat the injuries. Reassure the casualty. Raise the legs and keep the patient warm. Keep reassuring the casualty throughout this procedure. The psychological benefits of this are immeasurable.

△ Head low, legs elevated, then warmth and reassurance all help a person suffering from medical shock.

◁ *To help stop bleeding, raise the injured limb. This will reduce the flow of blood to the wound.*

▷ *Bandage the wound, having put a pad on to the wound itself. Do not overtighten, or this will cut off the blood supply to the limb.*

SEVERE BLEEDING

Severe bleeding is controlled by direct pressure to the wound site, elevation of the wound above the heart, if possible, and then padding and firm bandaging. If the initial bandaging does not stop the bleeding, leave it in place and put further bandaging on top.

HYPOTHERMIA

The human body reacts badly if the core temperature (that of the vital organs) drops below 37.5°C (98.6°F). A 2°C (3.5°F) drop is a medical emergency, a 5°C (9°F) drop can kill. We lose heat in the mountains through convection, conduction, radiation and evaporation.

COMBATING THE ELEMENTS

WIND, WET and COLD together are the worst combination, often with a relatively high air temperature. Prevention is far more effective than having to treat someone in a mountain setting. The signs of hypothermia mirror drunkenness: stumbling, confusion, erratic behaviour and slurred speech. Below 32°C (90°F) unconsciousness will occur. Often the best you can achieve in a mountain setting is to prevent further cooling. Any rewarming undertaken must be *slow* and *gentle*. The availability of a nylon emergency shelter will dramatically improve the chances of saving a

victim of hypothermia by providing instant shelter as well as keeping a party in a contained setting that contributes greatly to communication and morale. Several people inside one of these shelters will raise the temperature considerably.

△ *Hat and gloves, good insulation from the cold ground and a group shelter will keep an injured person warm.*

Maintaining life

▽ Salvation from the air. When a helicopter arrives, make yourself visible, stay still and wait until you receive clear directions about what to do.

The most important thing to attempt to do is stabilize the situation. This may be done by arranging shelter and insulation for the casualty. It is very important to give reassurance and warmth. You should encourage other members of the party to help you with this. The morale of the victim can be crucial. You should also keep a constant monitoring of vital signs, such as heart rate, breathing, skin colour, consciousness and alertness, and response. Should their condition start to deteriorate, shown up in one or more of these vital signs, immediate, appropriate first aid action should be taken. This appropriate treatment will ensure a victim's best chance of survival.

HELICOPTERS

In many parts of the world, mountain rescues are primarily carried out by helicopter. In all cases the most important thing to do if a helicopter arrives on the scene is to make yourself visible, secure all loose or light equipment, and do nothing unless specifically directed by the pilot or crew. Never approach an aircraft on the ground unless a clear sign has been given

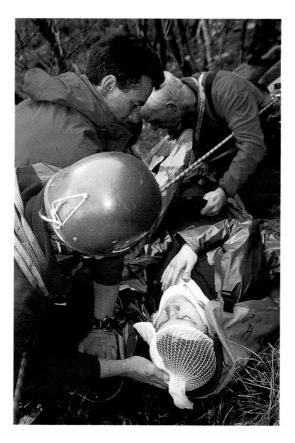

△▷ With the arrival of experienced medical help, you will be asked to pass on all the information you have about the accident and the casualty's immediate and present condition.

△ A small but well-planned first-aid kit and some basic skills are all that is needed to save lives.

to do so, then approach only in sight of the pilot and always from the front and downhill side of the aircraft.

EMERGENCY EQUIPMENT

When climbing on isolated mountain and sea cliffs you should always carry, or at least leave at the bottom of the route, an emergency shelter, first-aid equipment suitable for controlling severe bleeding, warm clothes and head torches. This will ensure you are capable of stabilizing the situation in the event of an accident and of going for help in darkness, if this is the best course of action. Do you go for help or stay with the victim? The big dilemma. Textbook solutions are rarely of any help in making the right decision. The choice hinges around whether anyone knows where you are and if they are expecting you back at a particular time. If they, are then the choice is easy; if not, you must do a mental "profit and loss"

account before making your decision. Start with the fact that if the victim is unconscious, then the justification for leaving them alone must be overwhelming. Finally, you are the only one who can decide, so disregard what judgements might be made by others after the event and keep a clear mind.

▽ A group shelter. These are light and cheap, and make all the difference in terms of warmth, shelter and morale when things go wrong.

First principles

Everyone navigates continuously and at a very sophisticated level, far more complex and sophisticated than mountain navigation. We are not taught to navigate around our homes, workplaces, or our cities; we learn it instinctively. Drop us into the mountains however, and many of us panic and promptly abandon all the skills we have used for years. Navigation is mainly science with a touch of flair and art in the closing stages. To navigate successfully you need to know and monitor the following.

▽ Navigating along ridges is easy when the visibility is good. In poor conditions it is very easy to end up on the wrong spur.

YOUR DIRECTION OF TRAVEL
This is determined by following a line feature, such as a valley or a ridge for example, by using a distant object such as a peak as a goal, or by creating an imaginary line feature by following a compass bearing (a compass bearing is an angle made up of a line between two points and a line to the North Pole). The good old Boy Scout idea of using the sun should be treated with caution. You are unlikely to make it to the sun and it moves all the time! Clouds may also blot it out at a crucial moment.

• TAKING A COMPASS BEARING

△ To get a bearing on the ground, simply point your direction of travel arrow on the compass at the feature you want to walk to. Then turn the compass housing until the compass needle lines up with the North sign. You will now have a bearing that you can read from the numbers around the outside of the compass housing. You will also have an imaginary line along which you can travel. Should the mist come down, you will still have a route to your goal. (See pages 72–5.)

• GETTING IT WRONG

You may well think that you know where you are when visibility is good, or you may not be worried about being too precise. This is fine – as long as the weather remains so also. But don't forget in your desire to get to your mountain crag that weather is fickle. It changes quickly. Do not get caught out if the mist does come down. If you notice the weather deteriorating, establish precisely where you are so that you can use the map and compass to navigate from the point when the mist really does set in.

△ Cloud forms very quickly in the mountains and can turn a simple journey into a complex navigational problem. Here a compass is not much use as the rocks contain spectacular concentrations of magnetic iron.

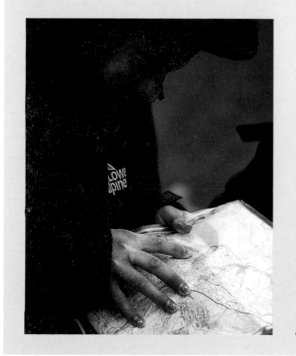

• MAKING THE LANDSCAPE FIT

Unless you have accidentally fallen out of the back of an aircraft at night, you will know where you are starting from and hopefully where you are going. However, a common mistake among mountaineers is that of making the landscape fit the conception of where they think they are on the map. For example, they may well be standing by a bridge over a stream in a deep valley, which fits with the map, but are prepared to overlook the fact that the stream is running the wrong way. This clue should tell them that it is the wrong bridge and stream! Neither map nor compass get things wrong (mostly, at least!). The trap of making what you see around you fit with where you think you are is convenient but may well be wrong. You must be rigorous with your navigation, especially when lost. Do not let clues as to your real whereabouts go unnoticed.

◁ Poring over the map won't help if you are determined to make the wrong landscape fit.

Time and distance

There are several principal methods of keeping track of distance travelled in the mountains. If you are working with reliable maps in country with obvious features then you can read the map and tick off the features as you pass them. This will enable you to know where you are all the time without necessarily knowing how far you have travelled. If you spend lots of time in the hills, you can build up a good picture of how far you travel over various terrain. Keep a mental track of distance during the day, filing the information in your head so you can recall it later in the day should it become necessary.

TIMING – NAISMITH'S RULE

To give you somewhere to start, there was a Scottish walking machine named Naismith who worked out he could pound through the hills at 5 km (3 miles) per hour plus 30 minutes for every 300 m (1000 ft) of ascent. Your job is to work out your own figures. If you have plenty of money, you can buy a reliable altimeter and when used correctly this can turn every contour line into a "tick off" point. All will be revealed later.

PACING

Another skill which is useful over short distances in poor visibility or darkness is pacing. You need to determine how many double paces (that is how many times one leg or the other touches the ground) you do in 100 m (330 ft). Do this over different types of terrain – a flat easy path, gentle incline, steep hill, rough broken ground and steeply down

▽ A perfect mountain scene, but it can all change very quickly. Keep track of where you are even in good visibility.

△ *Wild conditions with zero visibility and snow can occur in the mountains at any time of the year. Being ready for it is the key.*

△ *When things fall apart, change gear and accept that the journey home needs care and discipline. The more meticulous you are, the quicker you will reach safety.*

hill. Try to memorize your double paces for each of these, having tested them lots of times until you trust the figures and your ability to judge the terrain implicity. You can then count as you walk to measure the distance you have travelled. You will need to concentrate hard. This technique is not ideal if you have a mind that wanders.

THE PSYCHOLOGY

People fail to navigate accurately or get lost for two reasons, laziness or panic. Concentration, discipline and being meticulous overcome the first, and learning to be self-confident and developing the art of justified reassurance solve the second. Navigating in poor conditions is a lonely job if you are on your own with no one to bounce ideas off, or if you are the only member of a party who knows what to do. It is particularly testing if you are in a party surrounded by "doubting Thomases". An analytical and logical approach works wonders in helping you cope.

one double pace

shorter pace

one double pace

PACING

◁ **1** *Make sure you know how many double paces you take to every 100 m (330 ft) of travel. This way, you can accurately determine your location over short distances if visibility is very poor.*

◁ **2** *Bear in mind that your paces will be shorter going steeply up (and down) a hill. Therefore you will use more double paces for every 100 m (330 ft) covered.*

The map

△ Maps vary the world over but have a reassuring similarity in most cases. Take care to become familiar with the map before you need it in difficult conditions.

Most navigation hinges around a map, which may range from a rough sketch map in a rock climbing guidebook through to a near-perfect national map series epitomized by the Swiss Carte Nationale or the British Ordnance Survey. You should familiarize yourself with all aspects of the maps that cover the areas in which you plan to climb. This will include magnetic variation (see page 75), the legend, contour intervals and scale.

A PICTURE OF THE LANDSCAPE

A map is a picture of the land. The good ones are brought alive by contour lines and clear, easily understood symbols. Most maps point roughly towards the North Pole; the only reason for this is that the early cartographers lived in the Northern Hemisphere. There is no up and down in space. It is important to grasp a few vital pieces of information from a map you are not familiar with before you start navigating.

permissible footpath

site of battle

contour lines

ski route

glacier

first aid post

refuge-hut with keeper

téléphérique

camp site

dam

refuge-hut

cairn

marsh, reeds

viewpoint

coniferous trees

loose rock

triangulation pillars

boulders

cliff

climbing facilities

scree

mine shaft

outcrop

footpath

quarry

deciduous trees

rough grassland, bracken

SCALE

The first is the scale. This varies dramatically but the typical scale for mountain use is 1:50,000. This means that one unit of measurement on the map equals 50,000 of them on the ground. In practical terms, if using a metric scale, 2 cm on the map equals 1 km on the ground. The important thing is to be sure you know the scale and what that means to you.

CONTOURS AND GRIDS

Contour interval (lines of equal altitude) also varies a lot and can create embarrassing problems if you confuse it. Typically they are at 10 or 20 m (30 or 60 ft) intervals, get it wrong and your calculations will be 100 per cent out. Many maps have some form of grid or co-ordinate system which is unique to the country of origin. The good news is that in general they are made up of 1 km squares and the lines run pretty well north, south, east and west. The grid system is handy for estimating rough

● SCALES OF MAPS AND THEIR USES

Scale	Meaning	Use
1:15,000	1 cm=150 m	Orienteering
1:25,000	1 cm=250 m	Ideal for walking (very detailed)
1:40,000	1 cm=400 m	Mountain and orienteering maps
1:50,000	1 cm=500 m	Most common mountaineering map
1:100,000	1 cm=1,000 m	Cycling, holidays
1:250,000	1 cm=2,500 m	Motoring
1:1,000,000	1 cm=10 km	Map of country

distances and makes taking a compass bearing easier and more accurate, but it is primarily used to positively identify a position that has a unique number reference that cannot be confused with any other.

Familiarity with the map and its symbols is vital and the more time you can spend poring over it prior to going into the mountains the better. Trying to understand the map on a windblown col just as the unseasonable blizzard hits you is not the way forward.

Llachog mountain top

Dinas Bach

Main climbing crag – Dinas Mot

house platform

◁ △ *The map represents the landscape in two dimensions. Contour lines are designed to give an accurate interpretation of the shape and height of the land. You can see this clearly in the map and accompanying photograph.*

The compass

After the map, the compass is the most important tool the mountain navigator has. Knowing how to use it is essential for accurate movement around the hills and mountains in poor visibility. This is not an easy skill to acquire. It is important to practise in a safe environment until you are thoroughly conversant with all the techniques involved with its correct use.

MANY TOOLS IN ONE

The modern compass used by mountain navigators is made up of several different components. There is the floating needle which points to magnetic north, a protractor, a ruler and the flat plate that holds the rest together. From early childhood we have been told that the compass points north. In reality an unmodified compass needle will point through the earth at a spot in northern Canada, and worse than that, this point

▽ The compass is a versatile tool: protractor, navigator and distance measurer all in one.

moves all the time, albeit very slowly indeed. Fortunately people with more skill than us keep it all under control by making the compass needle sit up and swing and by publishing the magnetic variation so that with an incredibly simple adjustment to the compass we can pretend it is pointing to the North Pole.

USES OF THE COMPASS

The compass can be used for many useful navigational tasks. These are as follows:

① taking bearings directly from the ground
② taking bearings from the map and applying them to the ground
③ measuring distances on your map
④ finding north (using the magnetic variation)
⑤ setting the map to the landscape
⑥ working out grid references

Romer scale
100 m gradations
for measuring
distance

direction of travel arrow

magnifying lens

scale in mm

compass needle
(north end is red)

orienteering lines

read bearing against
index line

compass housing

base plate

orienteering arrow

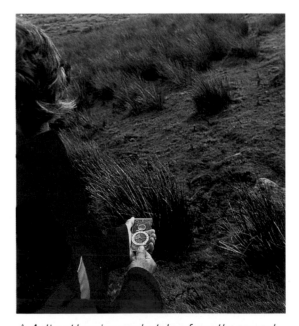

△ A direct bearing can be taken from the ground in the absence of a map, or the bearing can be applied back on to the map.

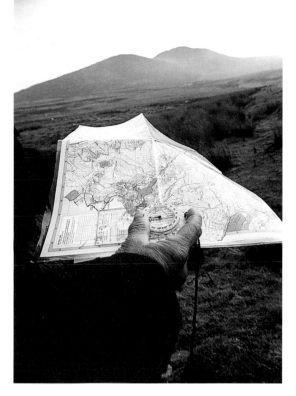

◁ *Most commonly in mountain navigation we take a bearing from the map (using grid north) and apply it to the ground (converting to magnetic north).*

▷ *Make sure you are using the right scale on the compass when you are measuring distances off the map.*

BEWARE DISTRACTIONS

Tiredness and stress will work against you being able to work effectively in close navigation. Make sure that you give it all your attention when necessary. This may mean cutting yourself off from the rest of the party while taking your bearing and working out your timing and pacing.

● USING YOUR EYES, EARS AND BRAIN

These are almost certainly the most important tools in navigation. Things are not always as they seem, particularly when they are distorted by mist or darkness. So always look, listen and think. If you are trying to find a stream in the dark, then listening for the stream is obviously more important than looking for it.

● GETTING IT WRONG

One of the most common mistakes in navigation is to get your compass bearing 180 degrees out. This means that you will be heading off in exactly the opposite direction to that in which you want (or need) to go. It is the easiest thing in the world to place the compass wrongly on the map, in effect getting the map upside down. Try to guard against this by double-checking the bearing before setting off. You might also take a quick note of the landscape and special features from the map that you should see when turning to face your bearing – if you can see anything at all, that is!

◁ *This compass is 180 degrees out – the red north-pointing arrow has been aligned to the south. This is a common mistake.*

The science

Is navigation a science or an art? It is probably a bit of both. It is certainly a skill that can be practised at home, or some other safe environment, until you feel confident enough to trust your life to it.

THE MAP

Taking information of your route accurately from the map is the basis of good navigation. What direction do I need to travel in, how far do I need to travel, and what am I expecting to happen are the three questions you must ask.

The last is perhaps the most important, as this will reassure you that what you are doing is right or alert you to the fact that things are going wrong. You need to interpret the map to know whether you are about to go steeply downhill or that after a kilometre you will run into a very steep slope, at which point you must turn left. This is map-to-ground interpretation and in its most sophisticated form can be used alone to navigate extremely accurately. When combined with other techniques as well, your navigation will become bombproof.

▽ *A featureless plateau can lead to massive cliffs, a big danger if your navigation is poor.*

△ *Keep your map safe and handy for reference. It is not much good to you at the bottom of your rucksack – worse still if it blows away.*

◁ *The top of this mountain ends in massive cliffs, a danger to any climber on a poor-visibility day.*

THE COMPASS

Compass bearings become important in navigation if visibility is poor or you think it may become poor shortly. The most common bearing is taken off the map and then applied to the ground. Imagine you are at a stream junction having walked up a valley heading for your crag. The mist is down and the crag is nowhere to be seen.

Place the edge of the compass plate on the stream junction on the map and then on the crag. Make sure the direction of travel arrow is pointing from the junction to the crag otherwise your bearing will be 180 degrees out.

Turn the compass housing around until the lines on the base of it are parallel with either the grid lines or the vertical edge of the map. Make sure that the orienteering arrow on the base of the housing is pointing north.

You now have a grid bearing which must be adjusted to magnetic before you apply it to the ground. Magnetic variation is different depending on where you are on the globe, so you must look on the map to find what it is. It will be either east or west of grid north and it will be increasing or decreasing annually. In most cases the map will be dated and the annual change will be recorded. Having established the variation, adjust your grid bearing accordingly.

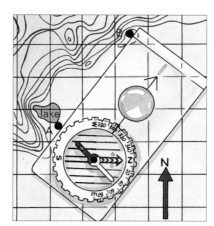

△**1** *Place the edge of the compass on the point where you are (A) and the point you wish to reach (B). Make sure the direction of travel arrow is pointing to your destination.*

△**2** *Turn the housing of the compass around until the lines on its base are in line with the grid lines on the map. Make sure the orienteering arrow is pointing to north on the map.*

△**3** *Add or subtract the magnetic variation (this will depend on which part of the world you are in).*

△**4** *You now have a magnetic bearing to march on. Turn the compass until the north needle lines up.*

● **MAGNETIC VARIATION**

Geographical North Pole
Magnetic North Pole
4°+
0°+
Yosemite National Park
2°+
0°+
Alps
Himalayas
16°+
27°+
Patagonia
Southern Alps

◁*Magnetic variation is hard to visualize because we are dealing with a sphere – the earth. The important thing is to read your map to find the appropriate magnetic variation figure and the rate of annual change.*

Using an altimeter

Like most pieces of specialist equipment, the altimeter certainly has a place in the armoury of the modern climber. But it is as well to know when and where to use it.

THE ALTIMETER

An altimeter measures the change in air pressure, so if you remain in one place it acts as a barometer and lets you know if the atmospheric pressure is changing as weather systems pass over you. If you climb up or down, it tells you how far you have ascended or descended. However, if the atmospheric pressure is changing dramatically as you are moving up or down, it will act as a barometer and an altimeter at the same time and will therefore be very inaccurate. Properly used and with a knowledge of the problems outlined above, an altimeter is an invaluable navigational tool. Altimeters use an aneroid or vacuum vessel which expands or compresses

1000 m outer ring

km window

adjustment for 1000 m ring

△ *Good-quality altimeters are expensive but very accurate if used properly.*

▷ *How much farther to the top of the climb? An altimeter will solve the problem.*

as the surrounding air pressure varies. This movement is then transferred either mechanically or electronically to an analogue needle or an LED display which is calibrated to read in metres.

With the arrival of watch-based altimeters, the cost of owning one has dropped dramatically, but do remember that you tend to get what you pay for. Altimeters work best if they are used over short periods of time and can be regularly reset at known altitudes. They are most useful for identifying obscure turn-off points in ascent or descent, so can be used for short periods using more obvious features as starting points. It is worth noting that every 1 milli-bar of atmospheric pressure change represents 8 m of altitude. Maintaining time and distance calculations in descent is notoriously difficult so this is really where they come into their own. They can be used either by setting them on a known altitude or they can be zeroed and then used in an absolute mode for however many vertical metres you wish to travel. This is often the best method in bad conditions as calculations are easier and less open to mistakes. Altimeters will never be a substitute for accurate navigation using more traditional methods, but as an extra tool to reassure and double-check in bad conditions they are invaluable.

◁ *Watch altimeters can be cheap and convenient but they are not always accurate. You get what you pay for.*

▽ *When the conditions are like this on the way home, an altimeter can make all the difference for safe and efficient navigation.*

The art

▽ *Getting to the top of the climb is sometimes the easy bit. Now you have to get home again! This is often where the navigation starts.*

To be a successful navigator you will need to be confident in your own skills. You will need to be able to juggle with lots of competing data, to sift through it and to prioritize it. You will also need to be flexible in your approach. No two situations are ever the same. Get in the habit of choosing your main skills that you will use for the situation you are in and call upon other data to back you up. For instance, you may choose to pace a short leg, walking on a bearing. But you might also work out how long it should take to reach your destination (probably only a matter of minutes in this instance), and use your watch to back up your pacing. This is where the flair and imagination comes in.

KEEP YOUR LEGS SHORT!

Navigation at this level will always be an inexact game but it is designed to keep the level of accumulated error to a manageable scale. Obviously, the shorter the navigational legs you undertake the smaller any error will be and you can relocate after each leg. So cut the journey up into small bits using the most obvious targets as way points.

USE COMMON SENSE

Keep a sense of scale. If what you are looking for is 500 m (550 yd) away from you to start with, then there is no point in crashing on looking for it for 2 km (2,000 yd). If, when you have travelled the correct distance on the correct bearing, you can't find what you are looking for, stop and have a think about where it might be. There will be many things to think through. If you are walking up a stream looking for a junction and have not seen one when your distance calculation is up, then it is most likely it will be in front of you a short distance. Continue on for a further 10 per cent of the original distance and you should arrive at it. If

bothy

corner of stream

foot bridge

forest corner
(attack point)

foot of crag

lake

◁ *Navigating via short legs in bad conditions reduces accumulative errors. Divide your journey up so that you find each point – foot of crag, edge of forest, foot bridge, stream and bothy – in turn.*

you find a stream junction too early then you have more of a dilemma. It may be the wrong junction if it is very early or you may just be travelling faster than you thought. Check the angle at which it joins the main stream: does it fit? It would still pay to carry on to see if there is another junction, but again have a definite distance in mind.

There is an old saying in navigation, "The tent will not come to you no matter how long you wait for it." You must find it, it will not find you. So you must be quite aggressive when you have navigated yourself near to your target, but make sure your search is logical and controlled; running around like the proverbial headless chicken is of no value to anyone.

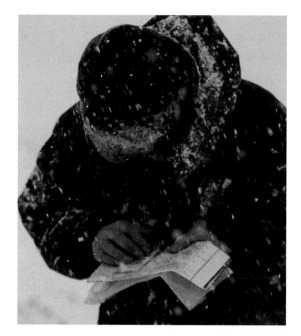

◁ *Taking a bearing in wet, cold and windy conditions can be very testing. It is often hard to achieve the accuracy you need in difficult conditions.*

● SEARCHES

In very poor visibility, it is essential to be totally accurate in pinpointing each stage of your navigation legs. You must find what you set out to arrive at. It is no good saying that the crag foot must be somewhere near, and then trying to continue on to the forest corner. Small errors at each leg may mean that you miss the bothy by hundreds of metres (yards), which in a storm could mean the difference between life and death. So, if you cannot find the foot of the crag after your pacing on a bearing, and timing, then organize a search to find it. You must assume that you are in the vicinity. Here are three examples of the type of search you might choose to use: the star search, sweep search and box search. Always make sure you know your way back to your starting point.

△ *You can adopt the star pattern with several people or alone, providing you return each time to your original spot.*

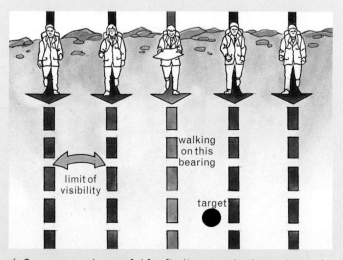

△ *Sweep search – useful for finding your tent or an injured person if you are travelling with several people.*

△ *Using the box search is a sure way of eventually finding your goal but it is tedious and very time-consuming.*

What do we mean by weather?

> *" It is obviously impossible to have a complete knowledge of the motion of a gaseous medium. "*
>
> *Seligman, 1936*

Weather is generally taken to mean the day-to-day effects of the humidity, precipitation, temperature, wind speed and direction, cloud cover and visibility at a specific place on earth. This is different to climate, which indicates the average conditions that weather produces over long periods of time in a specific place. It is the weather that we as climbers will be interested in – what is it going to do today?

Like navigation, weather forecasting is a mixture of science and art. It is important for climbers who venture farther afield to be able, through whatever means, to make their own judgements about it.

A CHANGEABLE MEDIUM

Weather by its very definition is changeable – in some places at certain times this may be a constant factor, almost hourly; in other places the weather may be more stable and predictable. With the development of modern physics theory, Seligman's statement appears to be more accurate than he imagined. This does little to reassure the humble rock climber wrestling with a weather forecast prior to committing themselves to a towering mountain route. However, despite the seeming chaos of the atmosphere, there is a lot we can do to up our odds against the weather. Armed with the best and most up-to-date forecast, a little knowledge, good observation and common sense, it is possible to win most of the time.

At various times all these can be good or bad for the rock climber, depending on circumstances. There is nothing like a bit of rain to allow you to rest!

THE GLOBAL PICTURE

The world's weather is driven by the sun. Because the earth is a sphere, various areas of it receive more or less radiation than others, creating dramatically differing temperatures, hot at the equator and cold at the poles. Hot air

▷ *A fine day in early summer and all is well in the mountains ...*

rises at the equator and descends at the poles, creating an area of low pressure at the equator and an area of high pressure over the Arctic and Antarctic. If only it was that simple. As the warm air flows towards the poles, it gets obstructed by the stable high pressure and some of it descends in the subtropical regions to create a band of subtropical high pressure. The semi-permanent Azores High that creates the wonderful climate of the Mediterranean is part of this system. Mid-latitudes are dominated by low pressure, which explains to some extent the climate of Northern Europe and Patagonia. To complete the circulation, air flows back from the poles to the equator, spreading over the earth's surface. As a result of the spinning of the earth, this air is deflected. The direction in which it is deflected is determined by which direction it is flowing and whether it is in the Northern or Southern Hemisphere.

△ ... until minutes later a summer snow shower has raced through, changing the situation dramatically.

● **GLOBAL CIRCULATION**

▽ The weather is a complex machine driven by the sun. It is complicated by the tilt and spin of the earth.

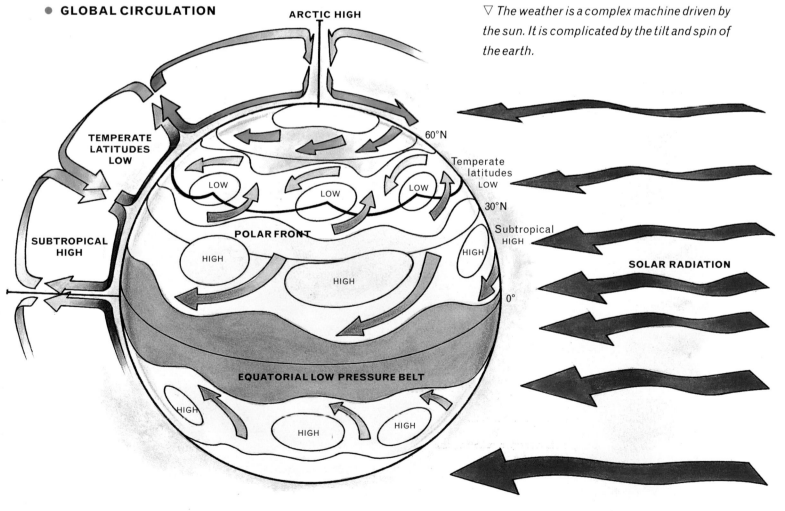

Major weather systems

Major prevailing weather systems provide clues to weather patterns in most parts of the world. These should be studied and absorbed for the place in which you plan to climb. These weather systems will contain air masses coming from particular directions, having travelled over certain landscapes or seascapes.

AIR MASSES

An air mass is a body of air in which the horizontal temperature and humidity gradients are relatively slight. Air masses develop the characteristics of the terrain they are in contact with or are travelling over. So, if a mass of air is travelling over a large area of warm sea it will warm up and become very moist; a mass of air that is stationary over very cold land will become very cold and dry. If two air masses of different temperatures run into each other, one will either bulldoze under or ski-jump over the other, causing air to rise.

ANTICYCLONES

An anticyclone is an air mass where air is converging at high levels and descending. It is an area of high pressure relative to its surroundings. Because the air is descending it is compressing, warming and can therefore hold a higher percentage of water vapour, so cloud will be limited and precipitation unlikely. Winds blow clockwise around an anticyclone in the Northern Hemisphere and anticlockwise in the Southern Hemisphere, and are generally light.

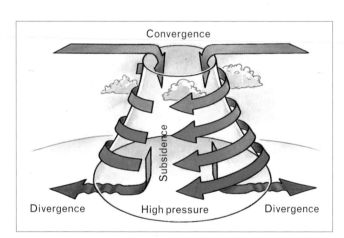

△ The air in an anticyclone is descending, compressing and warming. Cloud will tend to evaporate and winds will be generally light.

DEPRESSIONS (CYCLONES)

These are highly mobile air masses with divergence at high levels. Air rushes in the bottom and flows out of the top. This creates low pressure. The air is rising, expanding and cooling, therefore it can hold less water vapour so condensation results in cloud formation and precipitation in the form of rain or snow. Winds blow anticlockwise around a depression in the Northern Hemisphere and clockwise in the Southern Hemisphere.

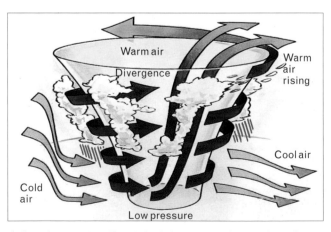

△ In a depression the air is rising, expanding and cooling. Water vapour will condense forming large amounts of cloud and shortly rain or snow will fall.

△ Sunny skies are associated with high pressure, but the wind is blowing hard. Low pressure is somewhere near, causing a steep pressure gradient.

FRONTS

These are the "battle areas" between diverse air masses. The name "front" was actually assigned to them in 1918 during World War I. They bring the wildest, wettest and most unsettled periods of bad weather.

COLD FRONT

A cold front occurs when a cold air mass runs into a warm air mass. The cold air moves along the ground surface pushing the warm air up. The rapid movement and steep slope of the leading edge causes strong lifting of the warm air, usually resulting in cloud formation, and precipitation associated with a cold front is usually confined to a narrow band of high intensity.

WARM FRONT

A warm front occurs when a warm air mass runs into a cooler air mass. A warm front usually moves more slowly than a cold front and the slope of the overriding front is very shallow. This ski-jump effect again creates cloud and precipitation which is spread over a broad area but is usually less intense than a cold front.

OCCLUDED FRONT

An occluded front develops when a rapidly moving cold front overruns a slower-moving warm front. The warmer air is lifted out of contact with the ground surface, cooling as it lifts. Cloud and precipitation result if there is sufficient moisture. The formation of an occluded front represents a breakdown of a frontal system. The weather associated with an occluded front may vary considerably in its intensity.

▷ *An occluded front.*

▷ *A representation of a typical Northern Hemisphere mid-latitude depression.*

◁ *A cold front.*

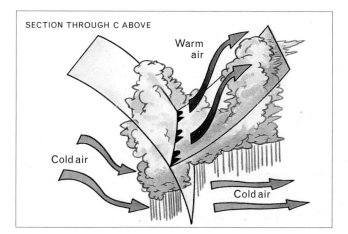

◁ *A warm front.*

▽ *Racing cirrus clouds give warning of a warm front on its way. It is time to think about descent.*

Interpreting weather charts

▽ Learn to read, understand and interpret weather charts. They are the key to good forecasting and medium-term planning in the mountains.

The weather charts we see in newspapers, on television, or coming out of fax machines are two-dimensional pictures of the atmospheric conditions at certain times. The chart is corrected to show sea-level pressure despite the altitude of the terrain it covers. There are two types of chart commonly published for use by the general public. A synoptic chart is a picture of the actual weather situation at the place named on the chart. This is an exact statement of where each weather system was at the given time. The second type of chart is a forecast chart and is how the forecasters imagine the weather systems will look at a stated time in the future. If you cast your mind back to Seligman at the start of this section you can see that these will be open to considerable error and therefore will require careful interpretation and conservative use. The newer the forecast chart or the more up-to-date the information you have to apply to it, the better.

ISOBARS

The chart is dominated by isobars – lines of equal pressure. These define areas of high and low pressure, the wind direction and, depending on how close together they are, the wind speed. The other major piece of information on the chart is the position and type of front associated with the various weather systems. A single chart is of limited use to us unless it is accompanied by information as to how fast and in what direction the various systems are moving, and whether they are intensifying or decaying. A series of updated forecast charts will help bring the situation alive for you. The other piece of knowledge that is vital is where each weather system has come from and the nature of the terrain it has travelled over before it gets to you. This varies dramatically from season to season.

● GETTING TO KNOW THE WEATHER CHARTS

To make your own assessment of the weather, you will need to become familiar with these charts and the weather systems that they indicate. You will also need to know where you can get hold of accurate information in the area in which you plan to operate. This may not always be easy. You will need to be able to understand the symbols and other data, and be able to make a reasonable guess as to what this may mean for you over the next 10 hours, or whatever your timescale is. Be prepared to change your plans if foul weather comes in sooner than predicted and try not to get caught out high up on a multipitch route when the rain and wind drive in!

▽ *Climbing big walls in the Greenland summer. Here it is important to get a view on what the weather may be doing before setting off to climb.*

The effects of mountains

△ *Cold temperatures high in the mountains mean snow will lie right through the summer, particularly on shaded slopes.*

Most weather forecasts are produced for the lowlands and to let people know if they should take an umbrella to work or not. Your job is to transfer this information into a mountain setting and to appreciate the differences. It will usually be colder and wetter, the wind will be stronger and there will be more cloud; or it may even be sunnier than the weather in the lowlands, in the instance of a temperature inversion.

TEMPERATURE

As you gain altitude the air becomes colder. This is because the pressure is less and so the air is less compressed. On a clear day the temperature will usually decrease by 1°C per 100 m (110 yd). If cloud is forming, this lapse rate is reduced to around 0.5°C as a result of heat being released into the atmosphere by the process of condensation.

TEMPERATURE INVERSION

This usually occurs after a beautiful clear night when the mountain tops have become very cold. This cools the air in contact with them. The air is now heavy and it rolls down the mountain side to pool in the valley floor, forcing the lighter, warmer air back up the mountain.

CLOUD AND PRECIPITATION

Mountains are cloudier and wetter than lowlands, because they force warm, moist air to rise, where it expands, cools and water vapour condenses.

▷ *This diagram shows the main effects that mountains have on weather in general. You can see how warm, moist air is forced to rise over the mountain barrier, causing it to cool and clouds to form. This may lead to rain or snow on the tops. Wind increases in speed and intensity as well.*

WINDWARD

Dissolving cloud

Saturated air cooling

Freezing level

1200 | -2°C
1100 | -1°C
1000 |
900 | Freezing 0°C level
800 |
700 |
600 | 1°C
500 | Dew point
400 | 2°C
300 | 3°C
200 | 4°C
100 | 5°C

ABOVE SEA LEVEL (METRES)

TEMPERATURE

Unsaturated air cooling

Dew point

Acceleration of wind

Turbulent airstream causing eddies to form over precipices

● WIND CHILL

Wind will have a dramatic effect on how warm or cold you feel. Even if the air temperature is a comfortable 10°C (50°F), a wind blowing at 32 kph (20 mph) will make it feel more like freezing or below. Any flesh exposed to this wind will go numb quickly. In the climbing context, this usually means your fingers.

WIND SPEED KPH/MPH						
64/40	-3/26	-12/10	-20/-5	-30/-22	-38/-36	-48/-54
56/35	-3/27	-11/11	-20/-4	-31/-20	-37/-35	-47/-52
48/30	-2/28	-10/13	-19/-2	-28/-18	-36/-33	-45/-49
40/25	-1/30	-9/16	-18/0	-26/-15	-34/-29	-43/-45
32/20	0/32	-8/18	-16/3	-23/-9	-31/-24	-40/-40
23/15	2/36	-5/22	-12/11	-21/-6	-28/-18	-36/-33
16/10	5/40	-2/28	-9/16	-17/2	-23/-9	-30/-22
	10°/50°	5°/40°	-1°/30°	-7°/20°	-12°/10°	-18°/0°

AIR TEMPERATURE °C/°F

△ Orographic cloud forming due to moist air rising, expanding and cooling, causing the water vapour to condense. As the air descends down the lee side the water vapour re-evaporates.

△ Perfect climbing weather above the low cloud and drizzle associated with a temperature inversion.

FÖHN WIND

LEEWARD

Dry air warming

Acceleration of wind through mountain pass

Dry air warming

TEMPERATURE	ABOVE SEA LEVEL (METRES)
-2°C	1200
-1°C	1100
0°C	1000
1°C	900
2°C	800
3°C	700
4°C	600
5°C	500
6°C	400
7°C	300
8°C	200
9°C	100

△ The wind on top of mountains may be two or three times stronger than that felt 1,000 m (3,000 ft) lower down.

Special considerations

Certain conditions that might be experienced in the mountains can at first appear puzzling or perhaps so obvious as to pass unnoticed. However, they may become significant as the day wears on – such as the effect of sunshine over a period of time.

WIND TURBULENCE

As the wind blows over the land and sea, it is slowed to a greater or lesser extent by friction when it comes into contact with the features on the surface of the earth. An exposed mountain top will therefore be in the stronger air flow. There are no rules to determine how much windier it will be as we gain altitude, as there are so many variables, but you should always assume it is going to be windier as you gain height or approach an exposed ridge. The mountains act like boulders in a river and create unseen rapids in the air. This causes spectacular turbulence that can lead to gusts far in excess of the actual wind speed. Not nice if you are teetering up a delicate runnerless pitch!

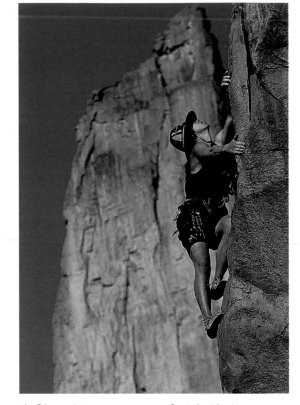

△ *Clear skies can seem perfect, but hot sun brings disadvantages such as sunburn, dehydration and heat exhaustion.*

SUNSHINE

High in the mountains the air is free of the dust, dirt and pollution that we experience at lower altitudes, so the effect of the sun is much stronger. This can greatly increase the problems of sunburn and dehydration.

ELECTRICAL STORMS

The complex mechanisms of thunderstorms are still not fully understood, but the dangers of them are very obvious. They are caused by extreme instability in the atmosphere either as a result of heat or very active cold fronts. Apart from the obvious danger of being struck by lightning, thunderstorms also produce very heavy rain and spectacular hail that can turn a

▷ *Wind in the mountains can dangerously cool you and can also be strong enough to knock you off your feet or blow you off your climb.*

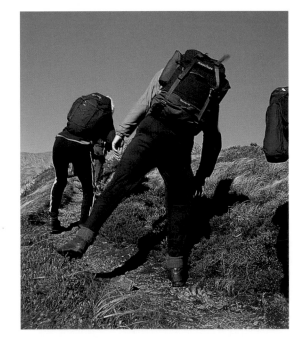

pleasant, sunny rock climb into a survival nightmare in minutes. Good planning and finishing your route as early in the day as possible will reduce the risk of being zapped. Storms triggered by the heat tend to hit in the late afternoon or early evening. If you are caught, then try and avoid high points, exposed ridges, caves and chimneys. If you are going to sit it out then the place to be is 100–200 m (330–650 ft) down the side of a ridge or face.

◁ *The ominous cumulo-nimbus and anvil cloud associated with electrical storms. Beware if you are downwind of it – it is coming your way!*

● ANABATIC AND KATABATIC WINDS

Air that comes into contact with the ground is heated or cooled depending upon the temperature of the ground. When it is warmed, the surface air will move uphill. This is known as an anabatic wind. The reverse is true when the surface cools the air in contact with it. Wind will tumble down off the hillsides into the valleys, causing frost hollows and belts of fog. This wind is known as a katabatic wind, and it reaches high speeds around high mountains.

ANABATIC WIND

Air rising due to intense solar heating

Cool air replacing heated air

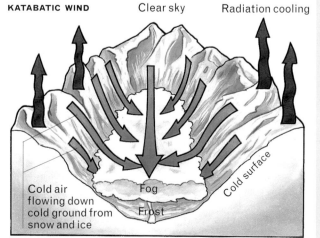

KATABATIC WIND

Clear sky

Radiation cooling

Cold air flowing down cold ground from snow and ice

Fog

Frost

Cold surface

Weather forecasts

▽ Perfect climbing weather associated with the semi-permanent high pressure that establishes itself over the Mediterranean in summer.

There is no end to the availability of weather forecasts in this age of information. We can get them in newspapers, on radio and TV, by fax and phone, on the Internet and by talking to the forecasters themselves in their offices and towers. Despite all this, we still spend most of our time moaning about how wrong they got it. You must remember that it is a forecast of what might happen and not a statement of fact. Armed with the forecast, you must put quite a bit of work into interpreting it and applying it to the exact location you are in. Thought is also needed regarding the possible changes in the atmosphere that might have occurred since the forecast was issued.

THE ATMOSPHERE

An important thing to bear in mind is that if the atmosphere is stable then forecasting is going to be very accurate; if it is unstable the accuracy will be greatly reduced and the chance of local variability greatly enhanced. Unfortunately, it is when things are unstable that we need good forecasts most. Such is life.

UP-TO-DATE FORECASTS

To stay on top you need as recent a forecast as possible for as small an area as possible, and if you can get hold of several from different sources you will get a much broader picture of what is going on. Most forecasts are general in nature and you will have to apply some of the information above to get a picture of what is happening in the mountains. However, in many areas of the world where climbing is a major sport, specialist mountain forecasts are produced and are extremely useful. In most countries a 12-hour forecast will be broadly accurate to around 85 per cent, but this accuracy drops off dramatically as you extend the time scale. A 4-day forecast will drop to around 50 per cent. Watch the development – the key to your own short-term forecasting.

FORECASTS IN THE FIELD

In order to accurately forecast changes in the weather we need to be fed new information. This is not normally possible when you are on a climb, so we need to observe continuously and make our decisions on what we see. You

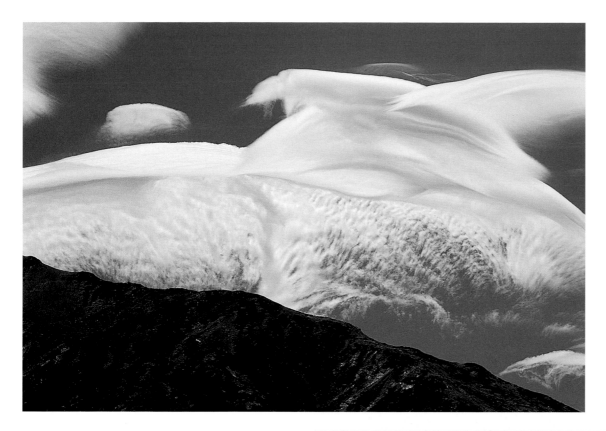

◁ Wild wave clouds provide a timely warning as a front approaches the Southern Alps of New Zealand. You have a few hours to finish your climb and find shelter.

▽ Thickening high cloud follows cirrus clouds as the front gets nearer.

need to decide on a timescale based on the seriousness of the situation. If you are on an easy rock climb with a straightforward descent, then it probably doesn't matter whether it rains or not. A very different situation would occur if you were already ten pitches up and about to traverse three pitches across into an inescapable gully system that will turn into a cascade if it rains. In this situation, before you commit yourself, you need to look back to the start of the climb and decide if the weather has remained the same or has deteriorated in any way, and if so, how much. Has the wind increased, decreased or changed direction? Has the cloud built up or has it dissolved? And more importantly, are the clouds growing vertically or all dying at a particular height? Clouds growing vertically indicate an unstable atmosphere with a lot of lift. This will often lead to storms and rain. Has the temperature risen or fallen? If there have been significant changes, then you must decide if you are happy to push on or not.

▷ Turbulence in the mountains can be severe. Ridges act like boulders in a river and cause acceleration and eddy effects in the air.

3

ADVANCED TRAINING

Rock climbing is being swept away by training hysteria. You only have to listen to a conversation at your local climbing wall or open one of the many climbing magazines to see just how much technical jargon and hype surrounds this controversial and fashionable subject. Gone are the days of pints of beer and pull-ups; today's climber speaks of plyometrics, intervals and super-compensation. To the average climber who aspires to improve their performance, the amount of conflicting views and information on training can prove overwhelming and, indeed, most climbers will use this as an excuse simply not to bother and to continue climbing in the same manner. This chapter seeks to clarify matters.

Opposite: *Rock climbing can be a serious business. Hard training and hard moves are the order of the day.*

Putting more in

The majority of climbers will experience a steady and satisfying rate of progress through the lower grades and up into the middle grades, simply by putting the time in on the crags and then using the wall on a fairly random basis during the winter season. However, regardless of our own individual base level of talent, we will all eventually reach a point where it simply is not possible to improve our performance any further without adopting a slightly more organized and self-analytical approach. Training does not mean taking the enjoyment away from climbing; it enables you to get more out as a result of putting more in.

A SYSTEMATIC APPROACH

Climbing is a complex, multi-faceted sport consisting of many subcomponents which contribute to overall performance. In your new systematic approach, you must think of climbing performance as a chain whose weakest links will hinder you far more than the stronger links will assist you. For example, it is

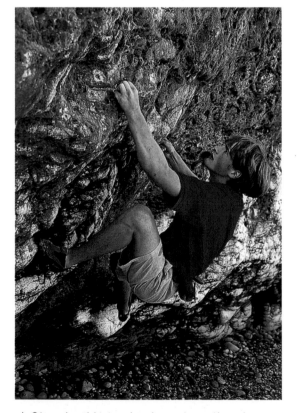

△ Steep bouldering develops strength and power and refines technique.

▷ For gaining mental control and crag skills, there's no substitute for sharp-end experience.

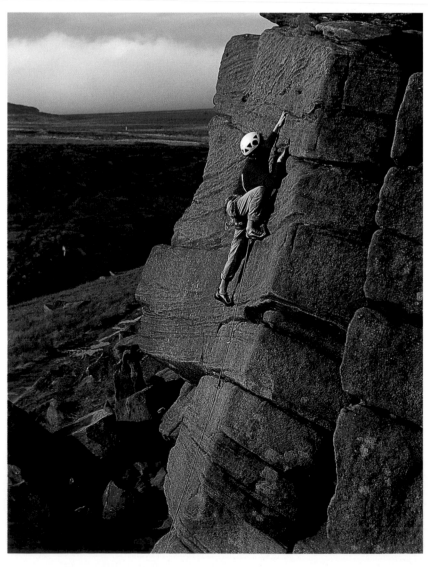

irrelevant how strong your arms are if your fingers are too weak to connect you to the rock. It is equally irrelevant how good you are at bouldering indoors when it comes to completing a long, arduous multipitch route on a remote mountain crag.

PRIORITIZE YOUR GOALS

Having examined your strengths and weaknesses, you must then offset them against your overall aims in climbing. It may be that you have no desire to be good at slabs and are content to dangle on overhangs from your marsupial-like arms for the rest of your climbing career – in which case, so be it, but never lose sight of the fact that the gaps in your performance will only widen as you hone in on your strengths and ignore your weak points.

PLAN TO BE FLEXIBLE

Fitting climbing and training in with all the other factors in your life can be a difficult task at times. Having determined what you want to achieve, both in the short, mid- and long term, you must then identify the key areas of training and practise what you will need to focus on in order to achieve those goals. Your approach should then prioritize those areas on an overall basis but not concentrate on them exclusively. For example, if your aim is to improve your ability to do long routes by training stamina and focusing on your on-sighting technique, don't become so channelled that you miss out on that long weekend's bouldering holiday with your friends. A balanced approach to climbing should accommodate minor day-to-day variations and changes of plan. After all it is unlikely that these deviations will disrupt the overall momentum of your program. If you are forced to take a week off in the middle of an intensive training phase, either through work or illness, worry not – it is incredible how often an unexpected break can motivate you to put that much more effort into the final part of the phase.

▷ *Your ability to remain relaxed on long, sustained routes can be significantly enhanced by specific endurance training.*

Periodized training

Those who wish to obtain maximum benefit from systematic training may wish to organize their climbing year into a periodized cycle. Periodized training is the term given to the use of a series of planned training phases (or microcycles) to provide momentum and emphasis towards a final peak. These microcycles may be anything between 3 and 12 weeks in length and they may show a specific bias towards a particular area of climbing fitness. For example, a so-called "strength phase" may consist of three sessions (or units) per week of bouldering and one unit per week of stamina training. The idea is that strength is emphasized and improved while endurance is simply maintained. If the endurance sessions were to be excluded then losses in fitness could be expected. Similarly a year's training (which can be regarded as a macrocycle) may be organized to achieve a particular degree of training emphasis, just over a longer time period. If your aim is to achieve a "balanced" performance peak (with equal emphasis on strength and endurance) then your yearly macrocycle could consist of four strength microcycles and four endurance microcycles. Alternatively, if your aim is to focus more on your strength and bouldering ability during the climbing year, then you may choose to conduct six strength microcycles and two endurance microcycles in order to prioritize the overall macrocycle towards a strength peak. Again, this may sound far too rigid and organized to those who are used to adopting a carefree, random approach to climbing, but remember that it does still allow you to simply go climbing and have fun!

◁ *A balanced climbing program could combine short power problems at the crag . . .*

▷ *. . . with longer endurance circuits on the indoor wall.*

Physical training principles

Climbing is not like weightlifting, and stored strength or endurance are useless unless you have the technical ability to utilize them. Gymnasts always incorporate a high skill element into their physical training and climbers are well advised to do the same. The age-old cliché that "the best training for climbing is climbing" still holds true up to a point.

PROGRESSIVE OVERLOAD

It is always tempting to start a new training phase by launching straight in and pulling as hard as you can on your hardest routes or boulder problems. Yet every prolonged period of training should start with a light foundation of easier climbing to prepare your body for the more intensive sessions that are to follow and to help you avoid injury. By increasing the overload (the term used to describe the level of healthy training stress) gradually and progressively, you will also avoid burning out prematurely and be able to stay at a peak for longer when the phase is complete.

UNDER-RESTING

Over-training has become a less popular term with sports coaches as it can act as a deterrent from hard training. The secret is to train hard but rest well. Ensure that you allow your body enough rest between training sessions; in doing this you must take into account not only the intensity of training but the type of climbing from which you are recovering (most climbers need to rest longer after strength training than endurance training). You must also take sufficient rest between longer training phases to allow complete mental and physical rejuvenation. A week of complete rest or light activity every two to four months will usually suffice.

◁ *Stay hydrated and energized both before and during climbing. Sports energy drinks and bars are a convenient solution.*

● LEVEL 4 SYSTEM

This system ranks training sessions according to their level of intensity or severity, level 1 being the easiest and level 4 being the hardest. A level 1 session barely allows you to break sweat and actually helps the body to recover by encouraging blood flow and gentle excitation of the muscles. A level 4 session would be an all-out fight, involving hours of gruelling training and climbing. The idea is that you use these rankings to assess what type of session you should have the next day, and in turn, how much recovery you need. You can also use this system to prevent yourself from going too hard in the early stages, and to allow you to attempt progressively harder sessions with correspondingly less recovery time as the phase progresses and you gain the fitness to cope. This process is known as progressive heightening.

Sample use of the level 4 system to achieve progressive heightening of a training phase (r = rest):

Week	Monday	Tuesday	Wednesday	Thursday	Friday	Saturday	Sunday	
Week 1	3	1	2	r	3	2	r	
Week 2	3	2	r	3	1	3	r	TRAINING LEVEL
Week 3	4	r	2	3	1	3	1	
Week 4	4	1	3	2	1	4	r	

Structuring your training

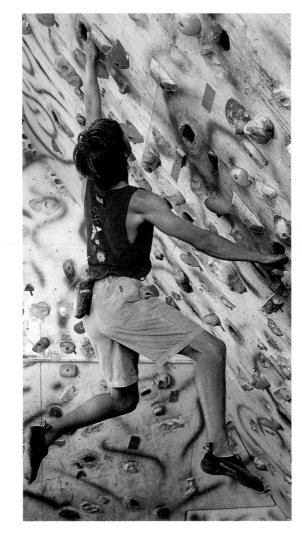

▷ *Dynamic moves on steep ground require a potent combination of arm power and finger strength.*

Another important training principle for climbing is to try as far as possible to structure your various types of climbing workout in the correct chronological order so as to maximize their respective training benefits. For example, many climbers feel that it is both possible and worthwhile to have a quality stamina training session after a relatively hard bouldering session (whether it is on the same day or the following day), whereas to attempt to boulder after getting completely pumped on longer routes would be a waste of time and energy. The rule of thumb is to precede longer, less intense climbing with shorter, more intense climbing although you will need to experiment to see if this works for you.

PHYSICAL TRAINING
In this section of the chapter we will presume, hypothetically, that we have all developed perfect climbing technique and supreme mental control. The reality could not be more different, yet if this were the case then further improvements in our performance could only come from training our body's relevant energy systems which provide us with specific local muscular strength and endurance for climbing. That is to say, we will be focusing purely on gaining stronger and fitter muscles and tendons for climbing, with less regard to how we should actually use them most efficiently.

STRENGTH AND POWER TRAINING
Strength and power are the physical components of climbing performance which are required to execute short, hard crux moves or boulder problems. The predominant muscle and tendon groups affected are those of the fingers, forearms, upper arms, shoulders,

● PHYSICAL SUBCOMPONENTS OF CLIMBING PERFORMANCE

SUBCOMPONENT	VARIABLES
Finger strength	Finger angles / hold type
	Contact strength / hanging
Arm strength	Arm position / move type
	Isometric (static) or Isotonic
	(dynamic)
Anaerobic endurance	Move type / rock angle
Specific aerobic endurance	Move type / rock angle
	Rest availability

△ In a campus board move, the arms work isotonically and the fingers work isometrically (see pages 102–3).

◁ Use strength and power training to help you tackle those hard crux moves.

▽ Finger strength is the most important aspect of overall climbing strength.

upper back and, to varying extents, the lower torso. Although leg strength is of great importance for climbing on low-angled rock, most climbers find that their legs are sufficiently strong to attempt the majority of climbs in comparison to their fingers and upper body.

CLIMBING STRENGTH DEFINED

There are two main types of strength in climbing. Crudely defined these are: isotonic strength, which is the ability to make controlled movements against high resistance forces (for example when pulling up), and isometric strength, which is the ability to hold static positions (for example, in the fingers when holding a hold, or in the arms when "locking

off"). It must be made clear that finger strength is by far the most desirable type of climbing strength; after all, the fingers are the last connective link in the chain through which all other forms of bodily strength are channelled.

CLIMBING POWER DEFINED

Power in climbing is simply the ability to perform extreme dynamic moves at high speed when required. In these situations, sufficient upward momentum must be generated not only to gain sufficient height to reach the next hold, but in order to create a state of "split-second weightlessness" within which to latch on to it. This technique is sometimes known as deadpointing.

Strength and power (1)

Having outlined the basic definitions and concepts of strength and power for climbing, the rest of this section will deal with the most popular methods that are used by climbers to improve this vital aspect of physical performance.

▽ Variety is the spice of bouldering! Train at different angles and experiment with different holds and moves.

BOULDERING

Bouldering is by far the climber's greatest weapon for developing strength and power in combination with climbing technique.

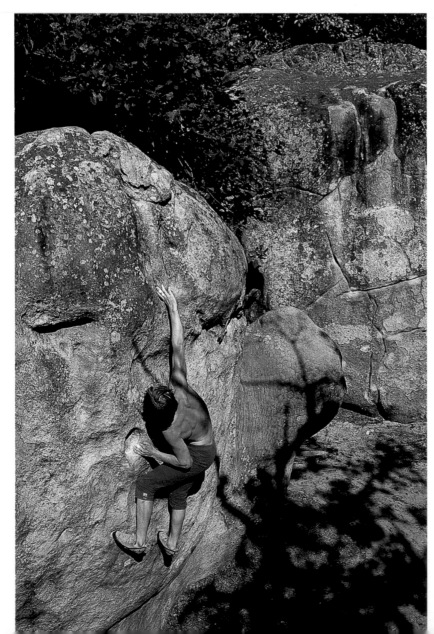

However, to obtain maximum benefit from your boulder problems it is vital to be aware of the great number of training variables that can be incorporated. For example, if your aim is to improve finger strength then don't climb on a wall that is so steep that it only enables you to use huge jug handholds. Conversely, if your aim is to work your arms then make sure you use large but well-spaced handholds and the smallest possible footholds. The most important principle of bouldering is to use different training facilities with different types of holds and surface angles and to vary the types of problems that you try.

This can be achieved according to the following guidelines:

① **Vary the handholds**
Full crimp, half crimp, hang (open hand), sloper, pinch

② **Vary the type of moves**
Pull-down, undercut, side-pull, reverse side-pull

③ **Vary the number of moves**
2–4 moves – for maximum strength and muscle-fibre recruitment
4–8 moves – for core mid-range strength work
8–16 moves – for the link between strength and anaerobic endurance

You can use a pyramidal structure with your bouldering, starting first with the shorter problems with harder moves and finishing with longer problems with easier moves in order to train in the correct order for optimum physiological adaptation. The most important thing is to take rests between attempts to maximize the quality of work.

SYSTEM TRAINING

Developed by legendary British training guru Matt "Smythe" Smith, system training is an advanced concept which enables you to apply systematic training principles to bouldering. It requires a specialized purpose-built training facility with the holds laid out in a uniform grid or ladder plan.

The idea is to be able to create boulder problems that enable you to repeat a series of identical moves in such a way that taxes a set sequence of climbing muscles repeatedly and to the point of absolute failure.

ISOLATION EXERCISES

For those climbers who find that they have a major deficit in either finger or arm strength, it may be worth performing some additional specific exercises that enable you to target your weak areas much more specifically than is possible with general bouldering. Note that these exercises should be used as a supplement (as opposed to a substitute) for bouldering.

① Finger isolation exercises

Deadhanging – This is simply a straight-armed static hang, performed most conveniently on a fingerboard with one or both arms (subject to ability) for a time duration of between 2–12 seconds. Select a hold that you can only hang from for 2–4 seconds and then work with it until you can hang from it for 8–12 seconds. When you have achieved this then move on to a poorer hold. It is important to experiment with different types of holds but beware of those that exert damaging "tweaks" on your joints or tendons.

② Arm isolation exercises

Pull-ups on a bar – The most basic exercise for building specific arm strength for climbing performed with one or two arms (and with additional weight if required) for between two and fourteen repetitions.

Travelling pull-ups – Perform as above, but move from one side to the other at the top of each pull-up.

△ *Footless bouldering is a superb high-intensity exercise for building specific strength and power.*

Bachar ladders – With this classic armblasting exercise, an overhanging rope ladder is tensioned off and climbed (with a foot for assistance, foot free or with additional weight subject to ability) for anything between two and fourteen repetitions.

Isometric locks – To train your ability to lock your arms statically, simply use a bar with one or two arms (and extra weight if required) and experiment by holding three positions (fully locked, 90 degrees and 140 degrees) using the same time guidelines as for deadhanging.

△ *A full crimp.*

△ *A half crimp.*

△ *An open-handed hang.*

Strength and power (2)

ote that those with a major overall weakness in upper-body strength may benefit from a more general strengthening program. However it is important to seek appropriate advice and to avoid exercises or repetition structures which may cause you to gain excessive and unwanted muscle bulk.

ABDOMINAL AND LOWER-BACK TRAINING

Climbing on steep rock requires a great deal of strength from the abdominal muscles, especially when attempting to lift your feet up to get them on to the rock. Certain extreme moves where you are stretched out a long way from your footholds also require what climbers sometimes refer to as body tension. This is the ability to keep your torso stable by using a combination of the abdominal and lower-back muscles. Of course, this type of strength will be developed simply by climbing on steep rock but those who consider that they have a major weakness in this area may wish to perform the following additional exercises.

Abdominals

Crunch sit-ups – Lie flat on your back with knees bent and then curl your torso up to your knees.

Hanging knee raise – Hang from a bar and lift your knees up to your chest, keeping your legs bent.

Lower back

Hyper extensions – Lie flat on your stomach, hands behind head, and arch your spine upwards taking great care not to overstrain.

△ *A laddering sequence on the campus board.*

◁ *A plyometrics sequence on the campus board.*

ADVANCED HIGH-INTENSITY STRENGTH AND POWER TRAINING

For those who have already gained a good base level of strength and power, the following exercises can be used occasionally and cautiously to help you gain higher levels of strength and power than are possible with conventional bouldering. But be warned, it is vital to warm up thoroughly and to treat these exercises with extreme caution.

Footless bouldering

The first and most obvious high-intensity exercise is simply to climb boulder problems on a steep wall without using your feet. This is a superb way to hone your strength, power and neuromuscular co-ordination for hard climbing.

Campus boarding

The campus board is a gently overhanging wooden board which is climbed footless using fingertip rungs that are spaced at uniform intervals. Developed by the late, legendary German climber Wolfgang Gullich, Campus boards are perhaps the most advanced and highly intensive training facilities that have

been used to date for developing extreme finger strength and upper-body power. There are three main exercises:

① *Ladder climbs*

Simply start footless and climb to the top of the board, using the widest possible rung spacings and without matching hands on each rung.

② *Touches*

Start from the bottom rung, pull up as fast as possible, touch a high rung, drop back down and catch yourself on the low rung again. Repeat, leading with alternate arms until failure.

③ *Plyometrics (double dynos)*

A highly advanced and specialized exercise which was converted from training principles used for sprinting to develop the elastic response in relevant muscles to negative climbing movements. Start with both hands on a high rung, drop with both hands simultaneously and catch yourself on a lower rung (absorbing as much energy as possible with your whole body) and then explode back up again to catch yourself on the high rung with both hands.

Endurance training

Controlling and reducing the dreaded forearm pump is the cornerstone of climbing long sustained routes. You may well have the strength and technical ability to do hard bouldery moves, but if your arms are so full of lactic acid by the time you reach the crux that you can barely hold on to a huge jug then your skills will be entirely wasted. Developing endurance for climbing is as much an aspect of technique as physical fitness. Learning to spot rests and use them effectively is a learned skill, and sometimes even the fittest climbers are caught out by those who have a better eye for a place or a position in which to recover.

Most climbers find it useful for training purposes to split the broad category of "Endurance" into two distinct areas.

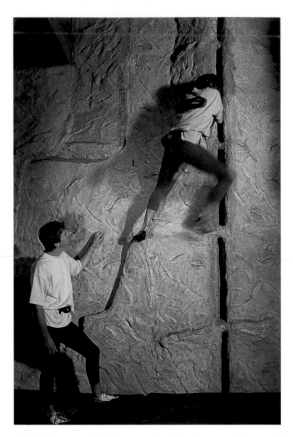

△ *Endurance training can be developed at the wall by performing traversing circuits.*

ANAEROBIC ENDURANCE

This applies to so called "middle-distance" routes which are sustained in difficulty and which are between approximately 15 and 30 moves in length. A typical anaerobic endurance route will have hard moves which will be less than your maximum bouldering capability but far too difficult to allow you to hang around and rest. Typically when you fail on an anaerobic endurance route you will not feel completely pumped with lactic acid; it is more likely that the sensation will be a combination of "pumping out" and "powering out"! Most routes at the average indoor climbing wall of 10–15 m (30–50 ft) in height will fall into this category.

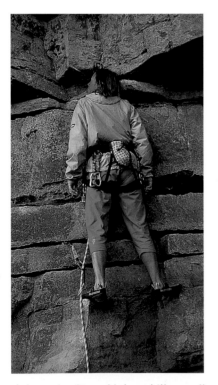

△ *Learning to rest takes skill as well as fitness.*

△ *Steep, sustained, middle-distance climbs demand high levels of anaerobic endurance.*

Stamina and aerobic endurance

This is the type of fitness that will be required on long (20–60 m or 65–200 ft) single pitch or multipitch climbs with individual moves that are of a relatively low standard. By definition, it is important that it is possible for you to rest and recover intermittently on stamina climbs as the effort required must be sustained over a long time duration, that is anything in excess of 3–4 minutes. During an ascent of a stamina route you must consciously attempt to "shake out" and flush the accumulating lactic acid out of your forearms. This may be done mid-move with a quick flick of the arm or alternatively by stopping on a rest or good hold for as long as it takes for you to feel more recovered.

▷ Longer climbs, in excess of 15 m (50 ft), require aerobic endurance – especially if traditional protection has to be arranged.

● ANAEROBIC AND AEROBIC
THRESHOLDS DEFINED

The terms "anaerobic" and "aerobic" refer to the ability of the body's energy systems to make use of oxygen to enable activity to be sustained during prolonged exercise. On longer stamina climbs, the body uses oxygen to take lactic acid (which is the bi-product of the energy production process) from the working muscles and transfer it into the blood stream in order for activity to be sustained. On the shorter, middle-distance climbs, the level of activity is too intense for this same system to be effective and energy must now be provided by a different, non-sustainable system which works in the absence of oxygen. In a process known as anaerobic glycolysis, a chemical called ATP is used and resynthesized within the muscles until such a point where lactic acid bi-products prevent the cycle from continuing. The inevitable result of this is that we fall off.

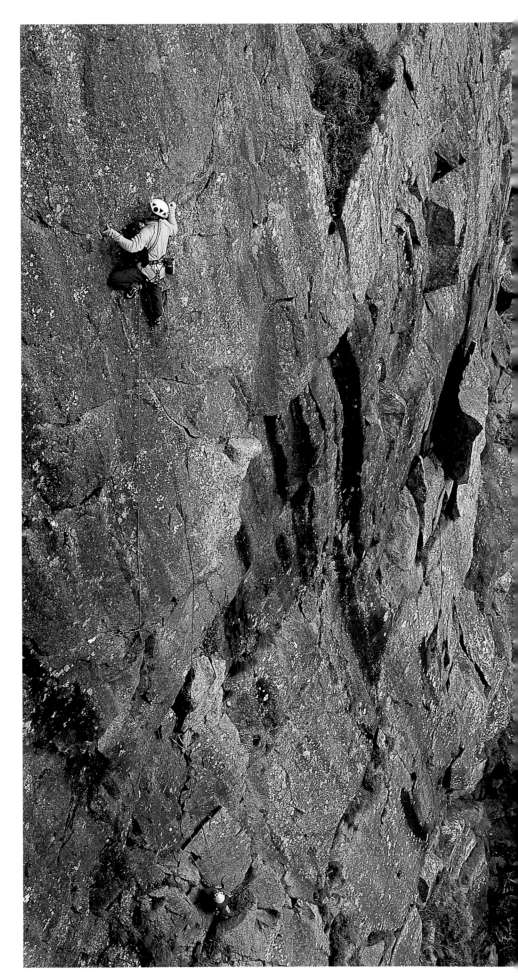

Anaerobic endurance

The best way to develop anaerobic endurance for climbing is simply to use routes or bouldering circuits of the appropriate length and difficulty in accordance with the criteria given earlier. However, it is important to gauge the difficulty of the routes so that you are able to complete them as opposed to burning out and falling off on every attempt. You must also allow yourself sufficient rest between climbs in order for you to complete a sufficient volume of quality work successfully.

TRAINING TO FAIL IS FAILING TO TRAIN

Forget the old and outdated cliché, "no pain, no gain". When it comes to anaerobic endurance training for any sport, there is an optimum level of training which must be sustained in order to tax and therefore extend the anaerobic threshold. If you climb until your fingers uncurl on every route, you will overtax your body and burn out before you are able to complete a sufficient volume of work. It is a simple equation: if the routes are too intense then you won't achieve sufficient volume; too much volume and the intensity is compromised.

INTERVAL TRAINING FOR ULTIMATE ANAEROBIC ENDURANCE

Achieving this balance between volume and intensity of climbing would be a nearly impossible task if it were left up to chance or guesswork. It is fortunate for us climbers that this

▽ *This classic 8a route requires anaerobic endurance.*

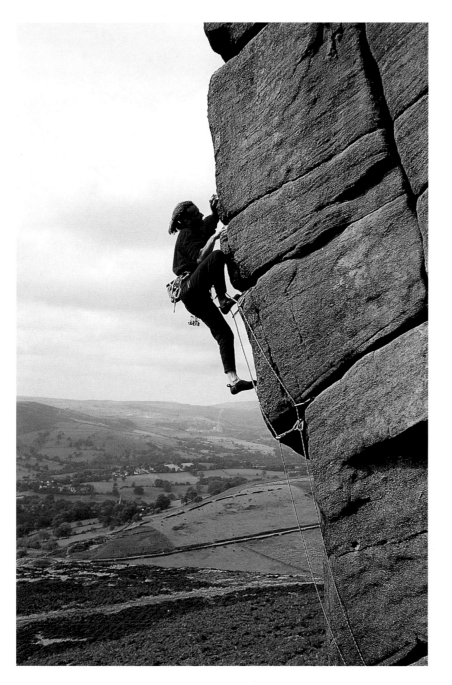

△ Anaerobic endurance also comes in handy for sustained sequences between rests on traditional climbs.

complex issue is well and truly understood in the more advanced world of mainstream sport. The French competition climbers were the first to realize that anaerobic endurance training can be summarized with one word: intervals. With interval training, you decide on a set route or grade of route, a set number of work intervals, a set recovery time (or rest interval) and then aim to compete all the work, but only just! – or perhaps to burn out only on the very last one. By definition, this means that the first few work intervals will feel relatively easy; but as the session progresses, you will start to feel under increasing pressure, until at the end it will be all you can do to squeeze out that final interval. Hence there is progression within the session and, ultimately, an intensity climax.

GUIDELINES FOR INTERVAL TRAINING FOR CLIMBING

The table below shows a sample interval-training structure for combining the length and intensity of climbing work with the appropriate rest times for anaerobic endurance. The idea is to start by using the higher values for rest times and the lower values for the number of intervals, and to achieve the lower and higher values respectively as you gain fitness over time. Remember also to vary the types of routes you use, and to use the crag for training as well as using indoor routes and bouldering walls.

● INTERVAL TRAINING

Suggested interval-training layout for the development of anaerobic endurance:

Work time	40 seconds	60 seconds	90 seconds	2 minutes
Approx. no. of moves	10	18	26	34
Rest time	1–2 minutes	3–5 minutes	4–10 minutes	5–15 minutes
No. per session	6–16	5–15	4–12	4–10

Adapted from D.R. Lamb, *Physiology of Exercise*, 1984

Aerobic stamina

When it comes to developing endurance for much longer climbs with easier moves, the process which must be simulated in training is that of flushing out the burning cramp that is induced in fatiguing muscles by lactic acid. In this type of training you must maximize the volume of work at all costs, by using routes of a sufficiently low intensity to enable you to hang in there for as long as it takes. If you make the mistake of training on a route that is too difficult and which requires near-maximum effort, the local muscles are forced to contract so hard that the surrounding capillary network is literally squeezed shut and, hence, blood flow is temporarily restricted. The result is that the process of lactic acid uptake and transfer is hindered rather than encouraged. Stamina climbing is all about the ability to recover on easier ground. So by training at a reduced intensity for an increased duration we can actually increase the density of the capillary network that supplies the local climbing muscles, the result being more efficient use of oxygen and dispersal of lactic acid, a process known as capilliarity improvement.

▽ *No situation will test stamina more than a long, arduous and committing pitch on a mountain crag...*

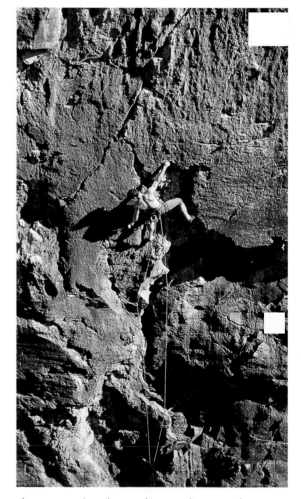

△ *...except perhaps a long, arduous and committing pitch on a sea cliff.*

● RECOVERY

As said before, the ability to rest and recover on strenuous ground should be regarded as a technique in its own right. Any of the techniques given previously should be employed to reduce the strain on the arms when attempting to "shake out", though particular attention should be paid to making shifts in body positioning as you recover each arm. For example, if you have two evenly spaced footholds at shoulder-width and two equivalent high handholds, when you take your left hand off to shake it you should shift your body to the right to align your centre of gravity directly beneath your right arm. This will enable you to hang straight-armed beneath it and thus use less muscular force to hold on. You should then shift to the left when you change arms. Breathe slowly and deeply and hang your resting arm down as low as possible. It is vital not to shake the resting arm too vigorously in your attempts to get the blood back into it as this will only cause instability in your body and a resultant strain on the active arm. A gentle and relaxed flicking motion will more than suffice.

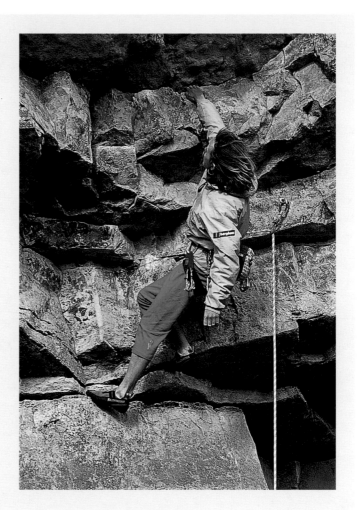

▷ "Shaking out" on a steep sport climb.

GUIDELINES FOR STAMINA TRAINING

With stamina training you should aim to climb for between 15 and 45 minutes at a time, on terrain which makes you feel moderately taxed, but in complete control. To make this possible, the climbing must be no harder than between approximately 30–50 per cent of your limit. For gauging intensity, a good rule of thumb is that you should be able to stop, chalk up and shake comfortably and hold a conversation at almost any point. You can also experiment by attempting some routes or circuits that have a fairly constant level of difficulty and others that have particular crux sections interspersed with good rests. Always aim to finish in a relatively well-recovered state, almost as if you could have kept going for an hour or two if boredom thresholds had allowed. With the shorter stamina routes or circuits that take between 15 and 25 minutes to complete, you may wish to repeat the efforts between four and ten times subject to your level of fitness or how hard you desire to train on that day. With the longer (25–45 minute) bursts, two to five repetitions will usually suffice. Note that one to three very light 15–20 minute stamina climbs can make an ideal active rest day to help you flush the toxins from your muscles and recover from previous hard sessions.

● STICK TRAINING

This popular method can be used when training stamina on a bouldering wall to help you simulate the effect of climbing on-sight on a route. The idea is for a partner to use a stick to point to the next hold or sequence of holds and for you to work out the most efficient way to climb between them. Obviously this requires good knowledge of your training partner's ability so you can set them a circuit of the appropriate standard.

ROCK AROUND THE WORLD

4

Rock climbing today is a world-wide passport to adventure. Low-cost air travel has made it easier than ever to be part of the international climbing scene. The experience of visiting far-flung and exotic destinations to climb can be as much, if not more, of an adventure than the sport itself. Exposed to new sights and sounds that threaten to overwhelm your senses, the climbing at times can almost seem like an excuse to be there. What follows is a brief tour around some of the world's most popular climbing playgrounds.

Opposite: *Rock climbing in Thailand – pure delight in a sun-drenched environment above a sparkling sea.*

Britain

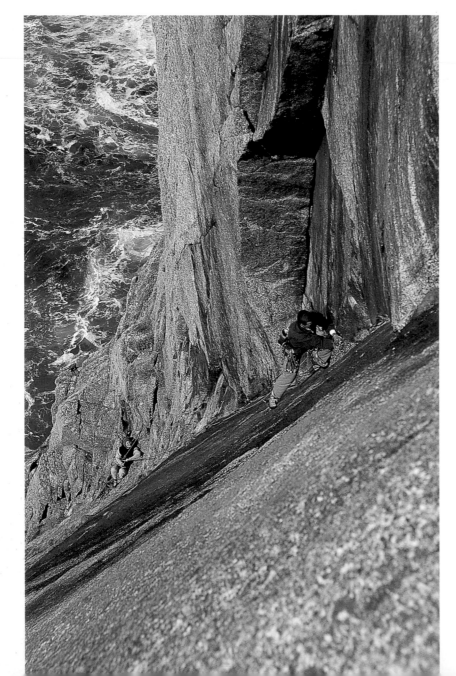

▽ *Lundy is a small island in the Bristol Channel. Around its granite coastline, it offers brilliant sea-cliff climbing of all grades. The island is approached only by boat or helicopter.*

Although small in area, Britain has a complex geology that offers a great variety of rock types and climbing venues, requiring a traditionally adventurous style of climbing using natural protection. Bolts are only used on a few crags, mainly featureless limestone. The unreliable weather is as much a feature of climbing in Britain as the wide choice and high quality of the routes.

THE SOUTH-WEST

Devon and Cornwall are home to marvellous sea-cliff climbing. Sennen and Bosigran are impeccable granite crags; the Culm coast offers plenty of excitement on less than perfect metamorphosed shale cliffs; and at Berry Head there are impressive limestone cliffs. Even with ideal tidal conditions, exercise caution if a heavy swell is running on any sea cliff. Most sea cliffs come into best condition from March through to autumn. Inland, Devon has granite climbing on the Dewerstone near Plymouth and the Dartmoor Tors, together with limestone at Chudleigh Rocks, a short distance from Exeter.

THE LAKE DISTICT

In the north-west of England is the Lake District National Park, where it is claimed rock climbing began as a sport in its own right with the ascent of Napes Needle in 1886. There are plenty of roadside crags in the accessible green valleys of Langdale, Borrowdale and Buttermere. Even the high mountain routes on Scafell, Great Gable and Bowfell take little more than an hour to reach from the road. Being a mountainous area, it is one of the wettest regions of England.

THE PEAK DISTRICT

Farther east, close to the cities of Manchester and Sheffield, is the Peak District – Britain's busiest national park. Climbing here is mostly on outcrops although some climbs reach 60 m (200 ft). Limestone crags can be found in sheltered dales and exposed gritstone edges stand stark against the otherwise featureless moorland. Gritstone gives the ultimate intense outcrop outing; jamming, balancy slabs and rounded breaks are all features of a day on grit.

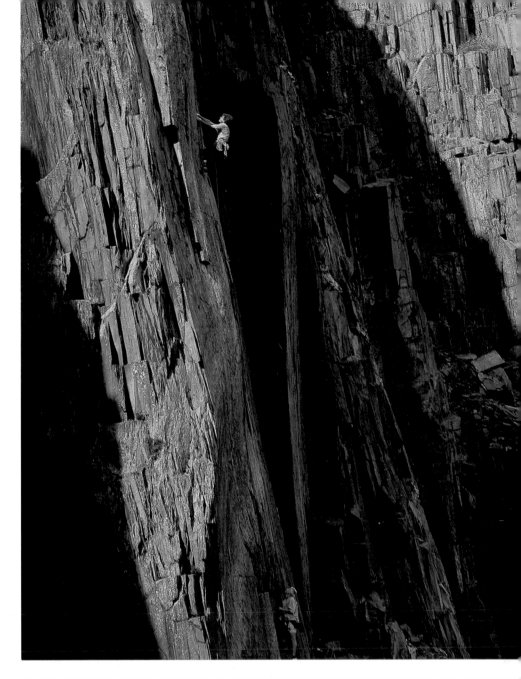

▷ *The Dinorwig slate quarries in North Wales provide a post-industrial backdrop to some fine climbing on a unusual medium.*

NORTH WALES

North Wales has a variety of superb crags all within a short distance of one another, from rocky mountain bastions steeped in history to modern sport crags such as Pen Trwyn with desperately hard climbing. Gogarth is a world-famous sea cliff in the north-west corner of Holy Island just off Anglesey. Many of the routes are affected by the tide and since some parts are colonized by sea birds during the nesting season, a voluntary access restriction applies during this period. The weather on the island is substantially better than in the mountains of nearby Snowdonia. Clogwyn du'r Arddu on the flank of Snowdon is one of the great testing grounds. An outing to "The Black Cliff" is akin to a pilgrimage for some climbers. Its dark gothic grandeur is definitely best sampled in the summer. The Llanberis Pass and Ogwen Valley have classic, naturally protected routes of all grades with easy access.

SCOTLAND

There are plenty of mountain crags offering idyllic seclusion, such as Creag an Dubh Loch, 300 m (1,000 ft) high in the southern Cairngorms, which requires a 2½ hour walk-in. Carn Dearg on Ben Nevis, the highest mountain in Britain, the Shelter Stone Crag above lonely Loch Avon and the tiered sandstone of Torridon's Beinn Eighe will all give memorable outings. Glencoe in western Scotland and Buachaille Etive Mor standing at the entrance to the valley are popular Highland venues. Skye is a beautiful, mountainous island out to the west with climbing on rough gabbro. To the north-east of Scotland lie the Orkney Islands and the famous 140 m (460 ft) sandstone sea stack known as The Old Man of Hoy. The sea cliffs around the Isle of Lewis in the Outer Hebrides have recently seen a great deal of climbing development. The best conditions for climbing are found in May and June; any earlier and snow may still be present.

△ *Strong natural lines on the imposing bulwark of Carn Dearg, Ben Nevis, are an obvious challenge to climbers.*

Europe

Continental Europe has some of the best climbing venues in the world. Most areas get warm, sunny summers that last for six months or more, so there is plenty of opportunity to spend long days on hot rock!

SPAIN

Think of climbing in Spain and sun-drenched bolted limestone comes to mind. There is no shortage of areas to choose from: Costa Blanca near Alicante and Benidorm with its holiday atmosphere; Costa Daurada, close to Barcelona; the atmospheric gorge of El Chorro, near Malaga; and the islands of Majorca and Tenerife are all popular destinations. Long, adventurous limestone routes can be found in the Picos de Europa. For a radically different experience, try pulling on the pebbles protruding from the conglomerate walls and towers of Montserrat or yarding up the "vertical potatoes" of Riglos.

▽ The Sierra Bernia in the Costa Blanca region of Spain is a Mecca for climbers who enjoy hot rock.

FRANCE

France is the home of "clip and go" climbing. Although it may lack a variety of rock types, there is something for everyone on its endless, mostly limestone crags. The Verdon Gorge in Haute-Provence is one of Europe's premier climbing areas. Its immaculate white walls are set in a position of mind-blowing exposure, a fact you become immediately aware of since the approach to most routes is by abseiling from the rim hundreds of metres above the river that winds along the gorge floor. Routes vary in length from one pitch to over 300 m (1,000 ft). It can be very hot in July and August and too cold for climbing from December to March.

Buoux and Ceuse are also found in this south-east corner of France: two top-quality sport-climbing cliffs that provide steep modern test-pieces. Further south, between Marseilles and Cassis, Les Calanques offers year-round sea-cliff adventures or cragging. The wooded sandstone area surrounding Fontainebleau, near Paris, is a Mecca for bouldering. Scattered throughout the beautiful forest are groups of fine-grained sandstone boulders. Each area has individually numbered problems and colour-coded circuits representing certain levels of difficulty that lead you from one problem to the next on a grand tour.

ITALY

The Dolomites, a group of limestone mountains in north-east Italy, provide classic and modern routes on an alpine scale but with straightforward access. A unique feature of this region are the Via Ferratas – exposed walkways and ladders protected by cables. Arco, close to Lake Garda, has better weather than the neighbouring Dolomites and offers plenty of roadside crags.

△ *The mountainous Mediterranean island of Corsica is a spectacular climbing get-away. Strangely shaped granite crags, such as Roccapina on the coast, are a stark contrast to the cliffs of its rugged interior.*

◁ *La Chapelle is a good medium-grade route in the Mont Blanc, Chamonix region of France.*

Between Aosta and Turin, the Val Dell'Orco in the Gran Paradiso National Park gives excellent granite climbing. It can, however, suffer from mountain weather, which can restrict access. The Val di Mello in the rain shadow of the Bregaglia Alps is another granite venue and is best known for its poorly protected slabs. July, August and September are the best months to visit these two areas. The Mediterranean limestone of Finale di Ligura, less than two hours drive from Nice, allows climbing throughout the year.

SWITZERLAND
Switzerland has many big limestone and granite cliffs set against dramatic mountain backdrops. A high concentration of routes are based around the Furka, Grimsel and Susten Passes. As with the other alpine countries, a lot of excellent rock climbing is to be found that involves glacial approaches. Many of the routes to be found here offer both bolt and natural protection.

● ESOTERIC GEMS

The compact limestone of the Frankenjura, north of Nuremberg in Germany, gives mostly difficult but well-protected climbing. In stark contrast is the excitement guaranteed on the sandstone spires and walls found in the Elbesandstein and Rheinpfalz (below) regions of eastern Germany. Knotted slings are the only protection allowed between occasional widely spaced bolts. The Czech Republic's most well-developed area lies 110 km (70 miles) from Prague. The conglomerate cliffs of Meteora in Greece, with its perched monasteries, are a spectacular setting for climbing. Sport and traditional routes, up to 14 pitches long, can be found. Spring and autumn are the times to visit.

The United States

It is difficult to grasp the scale and diversity of climbing in the United States. There is somewhere for every season and something to suit all tastes, from sport climbing at Wild Iris in Wyoming to big wall multi-day ascents in California.

YOSEMITE VALLEY

Yosemite Valley in California is the altar stone of American climbing and one of the world's best-known destinations. Famed for its big walls, it also offers good-quality cragging and bouldering. Walkers and tourists arrive in droves to view the glacier-carved features, such as the unlikely split mountain, Half Dome, together with the impressive 1,000 m (3,000 ft) sweep of granite known as El Capitan. This shield of rock has a mixture of

aid and difficult free climbs, inspiring climbers from both disciplines. Sometimes the speed of ascent is the most important consideration. In spring and autumn it is normal to see queues on the classic routes, such as The Nose and Salathé. To escape the heat and crowds, Tuolumne Meadows, less than two hours from Yosemite, provides a relaxing and scenic venue for shorter routes on granite domes dotted among pine forests, with views to the snowy Sierra Nevada.

In mid-summer the West Coast climbing areas provide cooler havens. Tahquitz, in the San Jacinto mountains, has a mixture of crack and face climbs on granite cliffs ranging between 60 m (200 ft) and 300 m (1,000 ft) in height. Neighbouring Suicide is a south-facing 120 m (390 ft) crag, ideal at the beginning or

▽ *Half Dome in the Yosemite Valley is one of the most popular big-wall climbing venues in the world.*

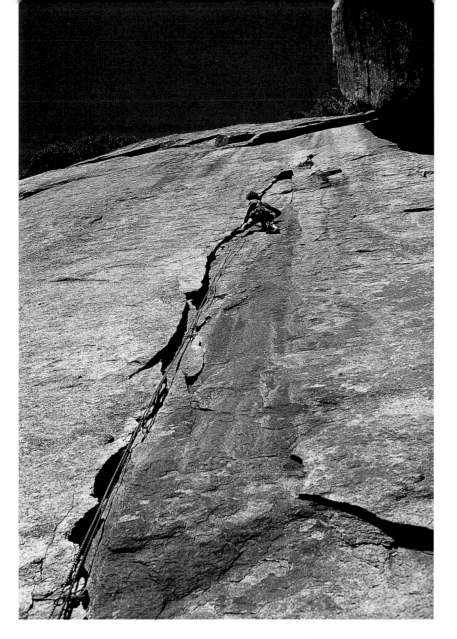

by the tree from which it takes its name. There are over 3,500 traditional and sport climbs on coarse granitic boulders between 6 m (20 ft) and 60 m (200 ft) high.

SMITH ROCK

Smith Rock in Central Oregon is a desert area with an unusual geology of soft volcanic tuff, forming complex multi-coloured towers and cliffs. It is best known for its single-pitch sport climbs. The mixture of crack, corners and face routes up to six pitches long rise above low-growing juniper scrub and sage brush. On the horizon, the snow-clad Cascade Mountain peaks can be seen. This venue is best visited in the spring and autumn.

◁ *Superb hard crack climbing can be found in the Yosemite Valley. This route is Outer Limits.*

▽ *Fantastic climbing in a great setting – Smith Rock in Oregon.*

end of summer. Set among coniferous forests in the southern Sierra Nevada, The Needles are a quiet summer venue. The climbing is focused on ten semi-independent summits. The characteristic bright yellow-green lichen-covered granite has routes on all aspects between three and twelve pitches long, giving some of California's finest crack climbing.

The steep airy granite of Lover's Leap near Lake Tahoe has a range of routes from moderate cracks to overhanging sport climbs up to 180 m (590 ft) high. Protruding quartz and feldspar dykes band the cliff forming small fingerholds to large ledges. Its north-west aspect offers welcome midsummer shade.

As Yosemite cools off at the end of autumn, many climbers head farther south to Joshua Tree National Monument in the Mojave Desert, where it is possible to boulder and climb through the winter and into spring. Many are attracted by its unique setting, characterized

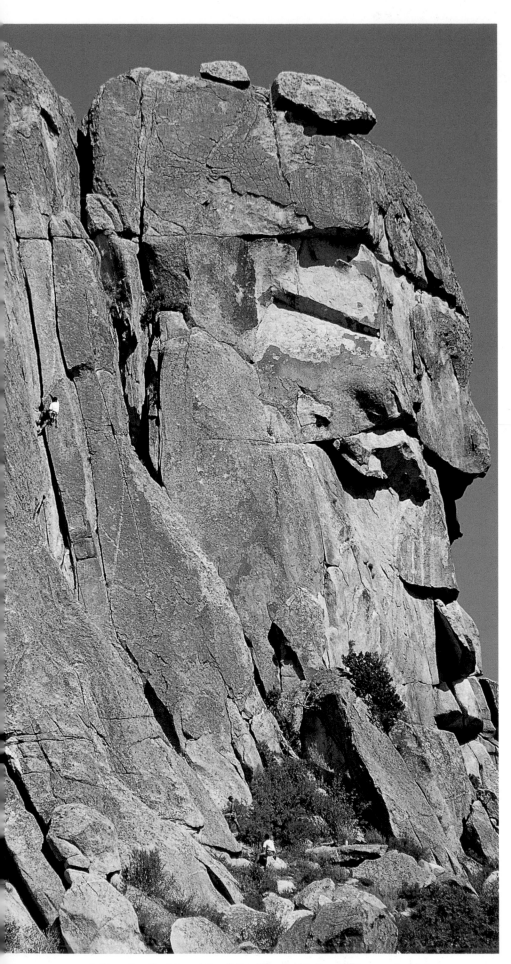

△ *Granite climbing at the City of Rocks National Reserve in Idaho.*

RED ROCKS

Red Rocks in Nevada is a West Coast sandstone venue and is a complicated arrangement of crags and canyons cut into a 900 m (3,000 ft) escarpment rising out of the desert. The climbing ranges from short clip-ups to long free routes. The rock can be friable and some descents are complicated. Only a short distance from the gambling showtown of Las Vegas, Red Rocks is highly accessible and most popular in spring and autumn.

On the edge of the Sawtooth Mountains, the City of Rocks National Reserve is Idaho's number one climbing area. A multitude of granite domes and pinnacles give mostly one-pitch sport and traditional routes. At an elevation of around 2,300 m (7,500 ft) it is a place to visit in the summer.

BOULDER, COLORADO

Since the city of Boulder in Colorado has so much nearby rock to climb, it has unsurprisingly attracted a large climbing community. The solid sandstone of the 300 m (1,000 ft) Flatirons, Eldorado Canyon and the granite Boulder Canyon are all within an easy drive. An hour to the north lies Estes Park on the outskirts of the Rocky Mountain National Park. Bordering this runs Lumpy Ridge with its string of accessible granite crags for short excursions.

Within the National Park, mountain routes with long but straightforward marked trail approaches give a remote feel to the climbing here. Some bolted routes exist but most require a full rack of natural gear, route-finding skills and an awareness of mountain hazards. Although not glaciated, snow patches linger into the early summer and violent afternoon electrical storms are common. Much of the climbing is on an alpine scale at an elevation between 3,000 m (9,600 ft) and 4,000 m (12,800 ft), so acclimatization is necessary.

June to September are the best months for a memorable experience on the quality routes of Spearhead, Petit Grepon and the area's centrepiece, the impeccable granite of The Diamond on Long's Peak. Also accessible from Boulder are the long, serious routes in the Black Canyon of Gunnison. The harsh Utah desert is home to the sandstone towers of the Canyonlands and Zion National Parks, revered among climbers for their sustained crack climbs in some of the world's most incredible scenery.

△ *Unique climbing on a unique geological feature – Devil's Tower, Wyoming.*

EAST COAST

The north-east United States has a landscape of gentle slopes with crags set among dense forests, the most popular being the Shawangunks. They can be reached in a half-hour drive north from New York City. The quartzite escarpment boasts over a thousand one-and two-pitch routes. Mostly naturally protected, they are characterized by steep juggy walls and roofs. Often hot and humid in summer, the Gunks are busiest during spring but perhaps best seen during the dramatic colours of autumn.

Recently very popular with East Coast climbers is the New River Gorge in West Virginia. Along the 24 km (15 mile) sandstone escarpment there is a mixture of more than a thousand single-pitch traditional and sport outings. Spring and autumn are the best seasons to visit.

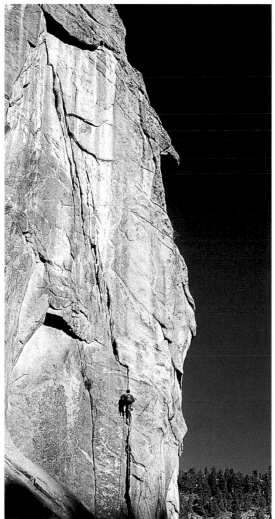

▷ *Climbing near Boulder, Colorado – an area that has attracted a large climbing community.*

Australia

Australia is the flattest continent on earth. It also holds some of the best climbing crags to be found anywhere. Unlike many northern hemisphere venues, heat can be a major problem.

ARAPILES

Australia is home to one of the world's best-known climbing venues: Mt Arapiles in Victoria. Only a half day's drive from Melbourne, a line of brightly coloured quartzite-hard sandstone bluffs above a group of pine trees that shelter the campsite gives classic climbs at all grades. With easy access, good weather and plenty of routes to choose from, it is a deservedly popular destination on the international circuit. The climbs rely mostly on traditional gear with the odd bolt for protection. Spring and autumn are the most popular seasons while shade from the searing summer sun can be found on the walls rising out of the numerous gullies.

In recent years, the Arapiles has had to share the limelight with a group of newly developed crags close by known as the Grampians, offering a variety of climbing styles and settings. The rock is again sandstone although unlike the Arapiles extensive bouldering can be found here and the weather tends to be cooler.

Mt Buffalo Gorge about 300 km (185 miles) north-east of Melbourne in the Victoria Alps is an altogether different experience on coarse granite. The style of climbing can vary from big walls to run-out slabs and flesh-tearing cracks. At an altitude of 1,500 m (4,800 ft), it is an ideal summer cliff.

THE BLUE MOUNTAINS

The Blue Mountains on Sydney's doorstep is a fantastic national park! In the midst of eucalyptus forest a multitude of sandstone canyons and escarpments offer dozens of crags mainly known for their short sport climbs. If only a limited time is available in the "Blueys", then Cosmic County and Mount Piddington are an ideal introduction to the vast amount of high-quality rock to be found. It can be wet and cold here in the winter so best avoided; spring and autumn give the most pleasant conditions.

Australia's premier sport-climbing venue is close to the town of Nowra. It is an ideal place in winter when you are feeling strong and the Blue Mountains are too cold. Short and steep, it has a high concentration of hard routes.

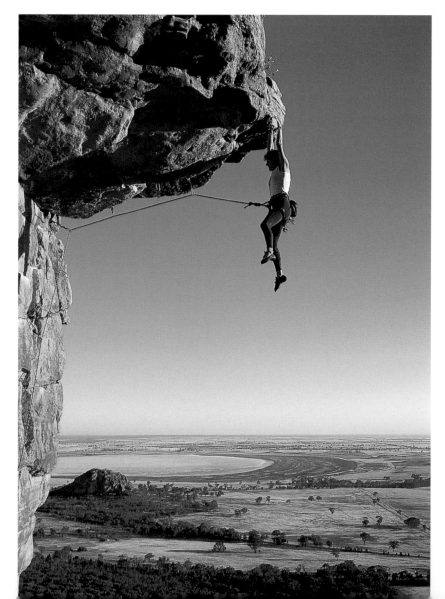

▽ *Hanging out down under on one of the Arapiles best known routes, Kachoong, offering big holds and plenty of exposure.*

Over the state border in Queensland, Girraween National Park is an idyllic venue and well worth a short visit. Set in prime bush-whacking country, the routes are mostly single-pitch with bolt protection on granite domes and curiously balanced huge blocks. At an altitude of 800 m (2,500 ft) the temperature can be below freezing at night.

About 1½ hours west of Brisbane is Frog Buttress, the ideal place to perfect your jamming and bridging techniques. Composed of rhyolitic columns up to 50 m (160 ft) tall, the crag is best-known for its continuous cracks and smooth grooves. There is very little fixed gear as most of the routes follow natural lines. Almost tropical in climate, it is definitely best to visit in the winter (June–September).

South Australia's finest climbing destination is Moonarie, about 400 km (250 miles) north of Adelaide, in the heart of the Flinders Range National Park. Situated on the crater rim of Wilpena Pound in an inspirational wilderness setting are routes of all grades up to 140 m (450 ft) long. Spring and autumn bring favourable conditions for climbing.

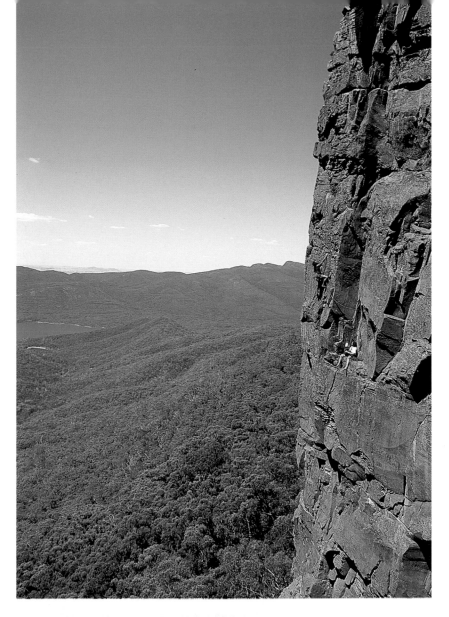

△ Mount Rosea in the Grampians offers long climbs high above lush eucalyptus forest.

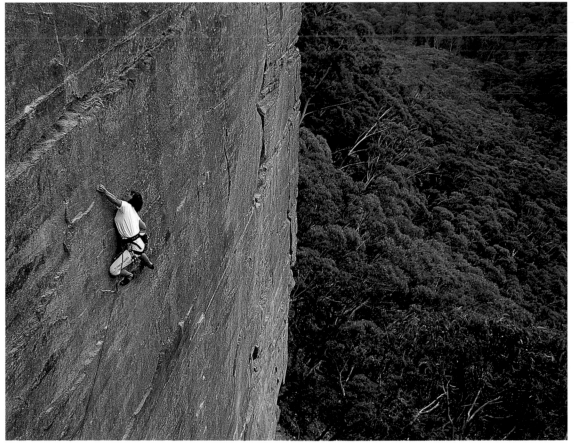

◁ Cosmic County crag is one of the many sandstone cliffs and canyons found in the "Blueys".

Asia and the Middle East

As well as being home to the highest mountains on earth, Asia offers great diversity to rock climbers, from the desert of the Middle East to the seaside crags of Thailand.

THAILAND

Thailand, the ancient kingdom of Siam, offers a paradise for climbers in which pocketed limestone walls draped with stalactites drop into the turquoise Andaman Sea. The main

▽ *Routes on the Ao-Nang tower, Thailand, can only be accessed by boat.*

△ *The aptly named Groove Tube is a gentle introduction to climbing on the Phra Nang peninsula, Thailand.*

destination for climbers is the Phra Nang peninsula, with around 300 sport routes within easy reach. Although the Phi Phi islands, a 1½ hour boat ride from Phra Nang, was the first area to be developed for climbing, the fixed protection has not been maintained and the poor condition of the bolts has meant a decrease in their popularity. Phra Nang's beaches can only be reached by boat, usually from Krabi or Ao Nang. Krabi is a 15 hour overland journey south from Bangkok or a three hour bus ride from Phuket. The peninsula has accommodation in bungalows across a wide price range; the cheapest bungalows can be found at Ton Sai Bay. In general the climate is a humid tropical one. Mid-November to the end of February is the best period for climbing. It can get very busy over Christmas and New Year.

▷ *In Hampi, India, there is a saying that every stone has a story to tell. For the climber it is like reading it in Braille.*

INDIA

Hampi, a holy village on the bare granite Deccan plateau of southern India, is one of the world's most unusual bouldering venues. It is an extraordinary landscape. Eroded into fantastic shapes, a confusion of huge stones sit piled up and precariously balanced in every direction you look. Many of them are strewn among the ruins that were once the capital of the Vijayanagar Hindu empire, destroyed in 1565. A sense of discovery and exploration still exists for the visiting climber.

CHINA

In southern China the area of limestone towers that rise out of the rice paddies around the town of Yangshuo have been tipped to become an important new climbing destination. A stunning limestone archway called Moon Hill is the main attraction for both climbers and tourists alike. At present the outcrop has 16 one- and two-pitch bolted lines. The middle of October to the end of February is the time to plan a climbing trip here.

JORDAN

The grandeur of the Wadi Rum desert in southern Jordan was first brought to the world's attention by Lawrence of Arabia. Prior to exploration beginning in 1984 to assess its potential for rock climbing, the region and its mountains were largely only familiar to the local bedouin. There are now some 300 routes of all grades on sandstone of variable quality. Original pioneers adopted a policy of using a minimum of fixed gear for protection to preserve the spirit of adventure. Recent excessive bolting has been seen as out of place in a wilderness area that has a timeless tranquillity about it.

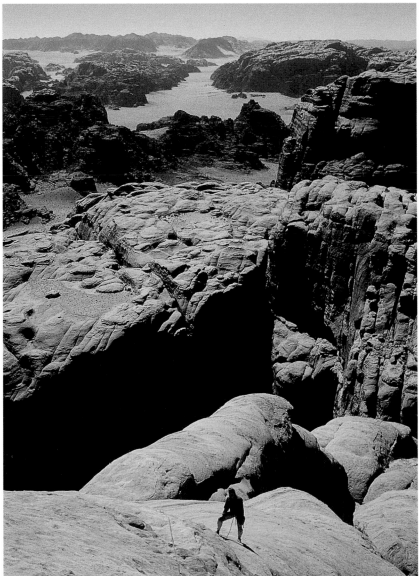

▷ *Climbing the Vanishing Pillar in Jordan with the Wadi Rum Desert in the background.*

Africa

It is only recently that rock climbing in Africa has been brought to the attention of international climbers. South Africa and Morocco are already popular destinations; others are still awaiting discovery.

MALI

The Massif des Aiguilles de Garmi, in the Sahel region bordering the southern Sahara, has emerged as the biggest attraction for visiting climbers. This striking collection of five sandstone spires includes the formation known as The Hand of Fatima. The great West African classic, The North Pillar, follows the pinnacled edge of the east face of the tallest tower, Kaga Tondo, in around 15 pitches. Descents generally involve abseiling (rappelling) and are equipped for 60 m (200 ft) ropes. An incongruous strip of immaculate tarmac passes through the arid plain just below the cliffs, making access easy. Camping is literally just off the road among boulders up to 15 m (50 ft) high, sporting numerous bolted lines. Hombori, the closest town, is 12 km (7½ miles) away dominated by the squat mass of Hombori Tondo, the highest point in Mali (1,155 m/3,789 ft). Some 140 routes have now been recorded. Many cliffs are under the stewardship of the local village and permission to climb should first be negotiated with the village chief. The Sahel can be ferociously hot so the best months to visit are December and January.

MOROCCO

Between the mountains of the High Atlas and the Sahara Desert in North Africa lies the Todra Gorge, a stunning natural feature of orange limestone standing some 300 m (1,000 ft) high and 30 km (20 miles) long. At its narrowest point it is only 10 m (32 ft) across. The gorge has hundreds of bolted single and multipitch routes with in situ belays. There is a regular bus service from Marrakech via Ouarzazate to Tinerhir (about seven hours) and then a taxi from here covers the remaining 14 km (9 miles) to Todra. Two hotels close to the gorge entrance not only provide cheap rooms and dormitory-style accommodation but also details of routes. The best times to visit Todra are March to April and September through November. Further superb limestone climbing can be found in the Taghia Canyons of the Central Atlas, with climbs of all grades up to 700 m (2,250 ft) long.

NAMIBIA

The dramatic 600 m (2,000 ft) granite plug of Spitzkoppe is Namibia's big attraction for climbers. This national monument rises out of the Namib-Naukluft Desert to a 10 m (32 ft) wide summit with vast views. The classic route

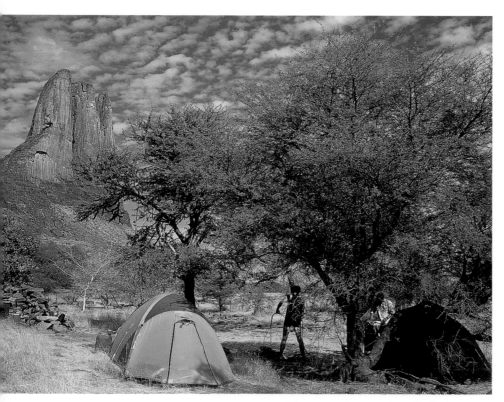

▽ Base camp below The Hand of Fatima; taking advantage of what little shade is on offer.

▷ The huge granite dome of Spitzkoppe in Namibia is a national monument and a big draw to climbers.

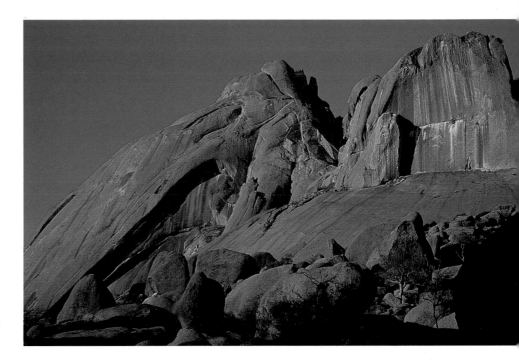

begins with a meandering line and even a spot of caving before six pitches of mid-grade climbing takes you to the top in about six hours. It can be reached by car with a bit of off-road driving and camping is allowed at designated sites, for which a fee is paid to the local community. Bring your own water.

SOUTH AFRICA

Since the end of apartheid a steadily increasing number of climbers have visited South Africa, bringing back reports of world-class climbing on sun-hardened sandstone. Table Mountain with its cableway to the summit dominates the skyline above Cape Town and is home to some great mid-grade lines up to six pitches long. A half-day's drive from there, Rocklands in the Cederberg Nature Reserve has incredible rock formations with sport routes in an exquisite setting and superb bouldering. A couple of

hours drive south from here brings you to the overwhelming rock walls of Wolfberg and Tafelberg. The main face of Wolfberg, about an hour's walk from the campsite, is nearly 200 m (650 ft) high with many multipitch traditional routes on perfect orange rock.

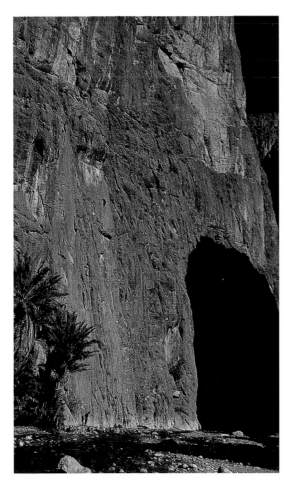

◁ The spectacular Todra Gorge in the Atlas Mountains of Morocco.

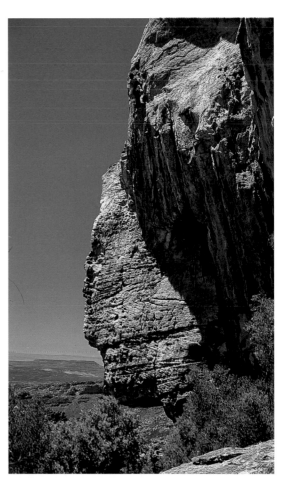

▷ South African climbing at its best – Rocklands in the Cederberg Nature Reserve.

Contact Addresses

UNITED KINGDOM
British Mountaineering Council
177–179 Burton Road, West Didsbury,
Manchester M20 2BB

Association of Mountaineering Instructors
c/o MLTB, Capel Curig, Gwynedd LL24 0ET

British Mountain Guides
Capel Curig, Gwynedd LL24 0ET

AUSTRALIA
Australian School of Mountaineering
166B Katoomba Street, Katoomba, NSW 2780

Australian Sports Climbing Federation
GPO Box 3786, Sydney, NSW

CANADA
Alpine Club
PO Box 2040, Indian Flats Road, Canmore,
Alberta T0L 0N0

UNITED STATES
American Alpine Club
710 Tenth Street, Suite 100, Golden, CO 80401

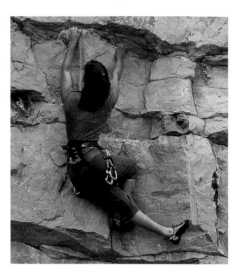

Acknowledgements

This book could not have been written without a team of writers who not only understand their subjects inside out, but have made decisions in everyday climbing and mountaineering situations based on that knowledge. To that end, the author has been extremely fortunate in having Nick Banks, Neil Gresham and Ray Wood as co-writers for this book. Thanks also go to Libby Peter for giving technical advice on many of the photographic shoots.

I would also like to thank all those who have either allowed me to trawl through their precious photographic libraries or assisted in providing specially commissioned photographs. These are Ray Wood, Mark Duncalf, Alex Gillespie, Nigel Shepherd, Chris Craggs, Tony Howard, Simon Carter, Graham Parkes, Nick White, David Simmonite and Nick Banks.

George Manley's clear and explicit diagrams have reached the parts that even these excellent photographers cannot reach.

I am grateful to the models Libby Peter, Sam Oliver, Edward Cartwright, Paul Houghoughi, Debbie Birch, Caroline and Simon Hale, Patrick (Patch) Hammond, W Perrin and Gavin Foster; and to Neil Adam and Roger Jones of Bethesda for the loan of historic climbing gear.

Finally, this section would not be complete without a word of thanks to Judith Simons at Anness Publishing and Neil Champion, who had the unenviable task of trying to tie up all the loose ends and deal with a crowd of itinerant climbers who insisted in disappearing to the four corners of the world at the drop of a hat.

The authors and publisher would like to thank the following companies and organizations for their generous help in providing clothing, equipment and facilities:

Troll
Spring Mill, Uppermill, Oldham,
Lancs OL3 6AA (for their harnesses)

Edelrid Safety Products
Shap Road, Industrial Estate, Kendal,
Cumbria LA9 6NZ (for their ropes)

DMM International Ltd
Y Glyn, Llanberis, Gwynedd LL55 4EL
(for their slings, karabiners, chocks, belay
devices and rock shoes)

HB Climbing Equipment
24, Llandegai Industrial Estate, Bangor,
Gwynedd LL57 4YH (for their slings,
karabiners, chocks and belay devices)

High Places
Globe Centre, Penistone Rd, Sheffield,
Yorks S6 3AE (for their T-shirts and sun hats)

Jagged Globe
45 Mowbray St, Sheffield, Yorks S3 8EN
(for their sweatshirts)

Regatta Ltd
Risol House, Mercury Way, Dumplington,
Urmston, Manchester M41 7RR
(for their fleece jackets and walking trousers)

Royal Robbins UK
16a Mill St, Oakham, Rutland LE15 6EA
(for their clothing)

Schoffel UK
16a Mill St, Oakham, Rutland LE15 6EA
(for their windshell and other waterproof
garments)

Sprayway Ltd
16 Chester St, Manchester M1 5GE
(for their windshells, fleece jackets and other
clothing)

Stone Monkey
Y Glyn, Llanberis, Gwynedd,LL55 4EL
(for their clothing)

Salomon Taylor Made Ltd
Annecy House, The Lodden Centre, Wade Rd,
Basingstoke, Hants RG248FL
(for their approach shoes)

Plas y Brenin
National Mountain Centre, Capel Currig,
Gwynedd LL24 0ET (for the use of their
climbing wall and other facilities)

Index

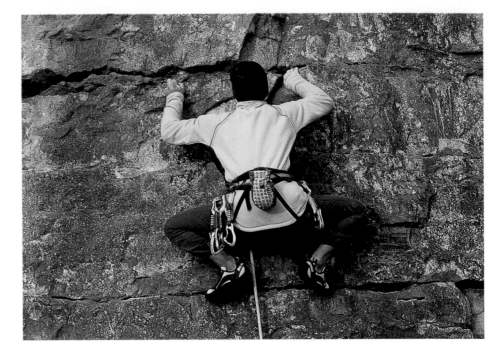

Photo credits

© Simon Carter: pages 120 and 121 t b.
© Chris Craggs: pages 114, 115 b, 116, 117 t b, 118 and 119 t.
© Malc Creasey: page 115.
© Alex Gillespie: pages 9, 14 br, 16 t bl, 18 l, 19 t, 60 b, 61, 62, 65 tl tr, 67 t, 69 tl tr, 74 tl bl, 77 b, 78, 79, 86, 87 tr and 113 b.
© Neil Gresham: pages 101 tl, 106 and 108 l r.
© Nomad: page 124 b.
© Graham Parkes: page 119 b.
© Nigel Shepherd: pages 10, 11 bl, 19 b, 25 b, 32 r, 64, 65b, 66, 67b, 68, 70tl, 72, 73, 74 r, 77, 80, 81, 82 b, 83, 85, 87 tl b, 88 bl, 89, 91 t c b, 112 and 125 t bl br.
© David Simmonite: pages 21 b, 22, 95 and 107.
© Ray Wood: pages 15 t, 17 t, 20 tl tr, 21 t, 23 tr b, 26 l r, 28 r, 31 tr, 32 l, 38, 60 t, 76, 88 t, 90, 93, 94 l, 99 tl, 100, 111, 113 t, 115 tr, 122 bl tr, 123 t and 124.